The Brooklyn Bridge Police Department

The Police of New York City, Volume 1

robert l. bryan

Published by robert l. bryan, 2023.

THE BROOKLYN BRIDGE POLICE DEPARTMENT

First edition. March 28, 2023.

ISBN: 979-8215104699

Written by robert l. bryan.

For Meghan - always the angel on my shoulder.

PROLOGUE

April 2, 1995, a date that will live in infamy. Wait a minute! I know what you're thinking. It didn't seem possible, but this guy managed to confuse the reader after only one sentence. April 2, 1995 is not a holiday and no significant event is associated with that date. For 99.9% of New Yorkers that statement would be correct. But for a very small, rare breed the date has tremendous significance. For former members of the New York City Transit Police Department April 2, 1995 was the day the music died. It was the day of the hostile takeover. In other words, it was the day the Transit Police Department went out of business.

For the better part of the 20th century the City of New York had been policed by three separate and distinct police departments. Just about everyone knew of the famous New York City Police Department, but far fewer people knew very much about the New York City Transit Police Department and the New York City Housing Police Department. The three departments had the same rank structure, and the pay and benefits were almost identical. Police officers in all the departments wore identical uniforms, with the exception of the department shoulder patch. While the NYPD policed the streets of the city, the Transit Police was responsible for policing the subway system, and the Housing Police handled the City's public housing projects.

I had been appointed to the Transit Police Department in 1981 and almost every subsequent year there had been talk of a police merger in the city, but the talk always seemed to just fade away. In 1994, however, merging the Transit and Housing departments into the NYPD became a pet project of the Mayor. The merger talks dragged on for about a year until the mayor played a trump card that had never been used in years past. The Metropolitan Transportation Authority was the New York State Public Authority that controlled and financed the Transit Police Department, and the MTA had no intention of ending its control of the department. The City of New York, however, contributed many millions of dollars each year for the operation of the Transit Police. The mayor simply put forth a very basic proposal. The MTA could keep the Transit Police Department, but they would now have to do it without the City's annual millions. Faced with this new economic reality the MTA was not so eager to have its own police department, and the MTA Board quickly voted to approve the police merger.

I went on to complete a productive twenty-year career with the NYPD, but like many other transit cops I felt the arrow pierce my heart when the Transit Police flag was lowered for the last time outside NYPD headquarters at One Police Plaza.

April 2, 1995 will always hold significance to me. I believed it had to be the most monumental day in the history of New York City policing. After all, despite the fantasies of the defund the police crowd, how many times does a full-service police department in the City of New York cease to exist?

I love cops and I love history, so when I saw the ad on eBay there was no question in my mind that a research project had begun. The ad was to sell an old police badge. I had seen many old badges, but I had never seen this one. The inscription on this badge was "Brooklyn Bridge Police." I thought I knew just about every obscure fact about New York City policing, but this was a new one for me. I never heard of a Brooklyn Bridge Police Department. There was no real description with the ad, and my initial thought was that it was probably some type of novelty item someone purchased at an amusement park. The chances of the badge being some counterfeit novelty only grew when I could find virtually nothing online regarding a Brooklyn Bridge Police Department. Then I stumbled upon the New York City Charter.

Prior to 1898 New York City consisted mainly of Manhattan. The other boroughs were all independent cities and towns. In 1898 the City Charter consolidated all of these cities and towns into the five boroughs that make up New York City today. This consolidation included all the government services, including policing. I was shocked to find out that April 2, 1995 was not the most monumental day in New York City policing. In fact, it paled in comparison to the policing changes that resulted from the New York City Charter. In total, eighteen police departments were disbanded when they were merged into the New York City Police Department. These defunct police agencies included the Brooklyn Police Department as well as departments representing other sections of Brooklyn, Queens and the Bronx. My eyes widened when I saw the name of one other department that was not a city or town. Disbanded along with the seventeen other departments was the Brooklyn Bridge Police Department. Such a department really did exist.

Researching the Brooklyn Bridge Police Department proved to be extremely challenging. Part of the problem was its short lifespan. The department was formed in 1883 and only existed for fifteen years until it was abolished by the New York City Charter in 1898. I could find very little information regarding the exploits and history of this department. In the end, I was able to piece together a history of the department's fifteen-year existence through exhaustively researching the New York newspapers of the period and letting the articles tell the story of the Brooklyn Bridge Police Department. I hope you find it as interesting as I did.

INTRODUCTION

I have been a New York City resident for my entire life. Such a simple statement should not be complicated, but it is. I live in the borough of Queens and for as long as I can remember anytime someone from my neighborhood mentioned "the city," they were referring specifically to Manhattan. Therefore, if an acquaintance from Queens asked me if I lived in New York City, I would answer negatively, explaining that I lived in Jackson Heights, Queens. On the other hand, while vacationing in California and asked where I lived, my response would be – New York City.

I suppose it should not be a surprise that identifying where I live should be such a complex issue. After all, the City of New York is a complex place, and its complexities have been present since the first settlement. As a matter of fact, it is the complexities and diversity of this city that serves to make it great.

The first native New Yorkers were the Lenape, an Algonquin people who hunted, fished and farmed in the area between the Delaware and Hudson rivers. Europeans began to explore the region at the beginning of the 16th century. Among the first was Giovanni da Verrazzano, an Italian who sailed up and down the Atlantic coast in search of a route to Asia, but none settled there until 1624. That year, the Dutch West India Company sent some 30 families to live and work in a tiny settlement on "Nutten Island" (today's Governors Island) that they called New Amsterdam. In 1626, the settlement's governor general, Peter Minuit, purchased the much larger Manhattan Island from the natives for 60 guilders in trade goods such as tools, farming equipment, cloth and wampum (shell beads). Fewer than 300 people lived in New Amsterdam when the settlement moved to Manhattan. But it grew quickly, and in 1760 the city (now called New York City; population 18,000) surpassed Boston to become the second-largest city in the American colonies. Fifty years later, with a population 202,589, it became the largest city in the western hemisphere. Today, more than 8 million people live in the city's five boroughs.

In 1664, the British seized New Amsterdam from the Dutch and gave it a new name – New York City. For the next century, the population of New York City grew larger and more diverse: It included immigrants from the

Netherlands, England, France and Germany; indentured servants; and African slaves.

As the city grew, it made other infrastructural improvements. In 1811, the "Commissioner's Plan" established an orderly grid of streets and avenues for the undeveloped parts of Manhattan north of Houston Street. In 1837, construction began on the Croton Aqueduct, which provided clean water for the city's growing population. Eight years after that, the city established its first municipal agency: the New York City Police Department.

Meanwhile, an increasing number of immigrants, first from Germany and Ireland during the 1840s and 50s and then from Southern and Eastern Europe, changed the face of the city. They settled in distinct ethnic neighborhoods, started businesses, joined trade unions and political organizations and built churches and social clubs. For example, the predominantly Irish American Democratic club known as Tammany Hall became the city's most powerful political machine by trading favors such as jobs, services and other kinds of aid for votes.

At the turn of the 20th century, New York City became the city we know today. In 1895, residents of Queens, the Bronx, Staten Island and Brooklyn–all independent cities at that time–voted to "consolidate" with Manhattan to form a five-borough "Greater New York." As a result, on December 31, 1897, New York City had an area of 60 square miles and a population of a little more than 2 million people; on January 1, 1898, when the consolidation plan took effect, New York City had an area of 360 square miles and a population of about 3,350,000 people.

In the Dutch era from 1625 to 1664, the first professional police department was created in New Amsterdam. Police officers formed a "Rattle Watch" where they used hand rattles and carried green lanterns on a pole as they patrolled the streets at night to discourage crime and apprehend criminals.

When they returned to their watch house, they hung the lanterns outside the house. It is due to this tradition that all precinct houses in the city today have green lanterns beside their front entrances.

Under British rule from 1664 to 1783, constables were charged with keeping the peace. They focused on such offenses as excessive drinking, gambling, prostitution, and church service disturbances. During the

Revolutionary War, the British appointed a military governor and employed citizen patrols to protect New

HISTORY · OF
CIVIC · SERVICES
IN · THE · CITY · OF · NEW · YORK
POLICE
No. 1
1658
On October 4, 1658
a paid Rattle Watch
of eight men to do the
duty from 9 o'clock
at night until mor-
ning drum beat was
established, the duty
being imposed upon
each of the citizens
by turns, and each
householder was
taxed 15 stivers for
its support.
Thief
Felon
The Rattle Watch

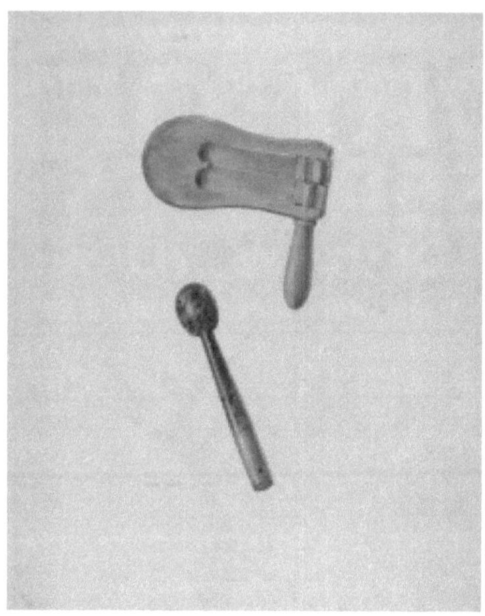

Some of the rattles used by the Rattle
Watch

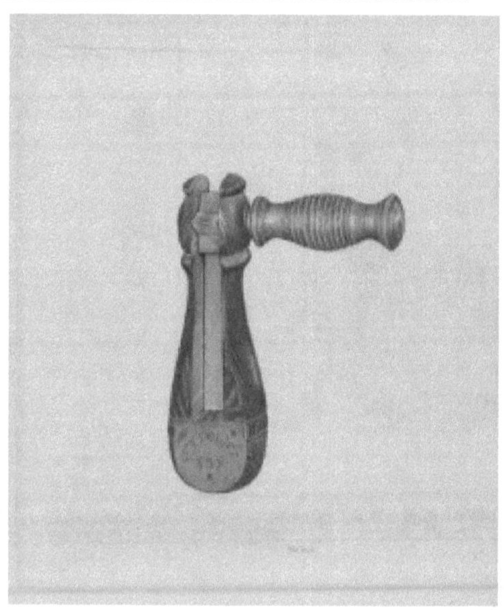

York City residents. After independence, New York adopted the London police model and established a paid professional police force in 1828.

The New York City Police Department traces its history back to 1845 with the passage of the Municipal Police Act, a law which authorized the creation of a police force and abolished the night watch system. At the request of the New York City Common Council, 1,200 officers were hired to staff the department, and the first set of printed rules and regulations was issued to the police force in 1845, with full uniforms adopted in 1853.

The New York City Police Department still had to undergo a lot of growing pains, and in 1857 that pain became very physical. June 16, 1857 was a significant date in the history of New York City policing, but not in a positive sense. Two rival police forces were operating at the same time in New York City—it did not end well. The unusual situation was the outcome of a corrupt mayor and opposing political parties heading the state and city governments and would eventually erupt in a bloody, all-out police brawl.

Democratic Mayor Fernando Wood misused New York's police as a means to guarantee election results and his power. Many of the police, meanwhile, took part in the graft and bribery common of the era. However, the recently formed Republican party, coming into control of the New York State government passed a law which disbanded New York's Municipal Police, and replaced it with a State-controlled Metropolitan Police force that encompassed the area of Manhattan, then independent Brooklyn, Staten Island, and Westchester County. Wood claimed the new police was illegal since it violated the principle of home rule and sued. A decision would not be made for months.

In the meantime, Wood's Municipal force and the State's Metropolitans were operating in the same city at the same time. The situation came to a head on the morning of June 16 when Daniel Conover went to City Hall to assume the office of Street Commissioner. He was appointed by Governor John King, an enemy of Wood and one of the chief republicans responsible for the new police law. The mayor objected to Conover's appointment, claimed the governor had no power to do so, and named his own designee for the office, Charles Devlin—a prominent city works contractor.

Mayor Wood ordered Conover removed from City Hall. This was done forcibly and with some violence. The incensed Conover then obtained warrants for arrest against Wood for personal injury and inciting a riot which was given to a Metropolitan Police captain to execute. The captain went to City Hall and was admitted into Wood's private office. The mayor, holding his staff of office, refused to recognize the captain as an officer of the law. The officer attempted to seize the mayor, but since Wood had filled City Hall with his Municipals, he found himself removed from the mayor's office and deposited into the hallway.

Mayor Wood reinforced City Hall with several hundred Municipals and locked the building. At 3:30 pm, a phalanx of fifty Metropolitans marching two abreast on City Hall. The Metropolitans were in full uniform with frock coats and newly minted badges. Each of their plug hats was decorated with a ribbon labeled "Metropolitan Police" and their officer number. They brandished batons—nearly 12-inch clubs which were their primary tools for law enforcement. Coroner Frederick W. Perry was to deliver the warrant and arrest the mayor.

A mob of Wood supporters heckled the Metropolitans while cheering for Fernando Wood. Some shouted, "Here they come; pitch into the sons of bitches." Some broke off branches to use as weapons. Some brandished brickbats. Some gathered stones. And some climbed into the park's trees for a better view.

Shoving the crowd aside, the Metropolitans made their way toward the rear entrance of City Hall. As they pushed up the twenty steps to the stoop of the entryway, they encountered about thirty Municipals guarding the entrance. Shoving and arguing began, then, out of a side door rushed a reinforcement of Municipals brandishing their clubs. The Metropolitans were flanked front and side with an angry mob behind them. They did not stand a chance.

The Metropolitans were driven back down the stairs, but not from the field. They re-formed and charged up the stairs to take the doors by storm. Coroner Perry almost made it inside before he was roughly pushed off the stoop. Again, the Municipals, in far superior numbers and having tactical advantage, attacked. The Metropolitans fled the field with the Municipals and the mob chasing after them.

Wood may have won the battle but not the war. The violence was settled later in the day by the 7th regiment of the National Guard. The mayor was arrested then quickly released. Wood and the governor called a truce and agreed to let both forces patrol the city uninterrupted until the mayor's appeal was settled in court. Wood's Municipal Police were finally disbanded when the New York Court of Appeals ruled in the State's favor on July 2. [1]

THE BROOKLYN BRIDGE

The Brooklyn Bridge, constructed between 1870 and 1883, is perhaps the most storied and most famous bridge in the world. With a main span of 1,595.5 feet, it was the longest suspension bridge in the world from its opening until 1903, and the first steel-wire suspension bridge ever built.

The bridge remains an essential stop for all New York City sightseers, who stroll its pedestrian path between Manhattan's Civic Center and the charming residential enclave of Brooklyn Heights. The Brooklyn Bridge changed New York forever when it was built and remains an essential transport link today. But whose idea was it, and how did it get built?

Even by the middle of the 19th century, there were few bridges over major rivers; goods were floated across on barges, and people rode ferries. In 1841, German engineer John A. Roebling began producing wire rope strong enough to support bridge roadways and was hired to produce a number of river crossings, the first over the Monongahela River in Pittsburgh in 1845. After a number of successful commissions, he built a large wire rope plant in Trenton, New Jersey.

In the following decade, Roebling designed a railroad bridge over the Ohio River between Cincinnati, OH, and Covington, KY, which resembles a smaller version of the Brooklyn Bridge. He first conceived of the Brooklyn span in 1852, but it took him more than 15 years to secure approvals for it, as the Civil War, among other occurrences, sapped capital and materials. Such a crossing was becoming crucial, because in that era, winters were colder, and barges and boats found the ice-choked river difficult to navigate.

In 1867, aided by a particularly harsh winter, Roebling enlisted the aid of prominent businessman William Kingsley and state Senator Henry Murphy, and after two years of negotiations with the city and state, the East River Bridge was approved in 1869. Fourteen years of construction commenced. John Roebling died from a tetanus-infected wound at a pier accident that year, at the age of 63, but his son, Washington, working from voluminous notes his father had produced, completed the project.

Much of the initial work on the bridge was done in the riverbed, where the foundations of the bridge towers were built using caissons — large airtight boxes or cylinders in which men, breathing compressed air, dug the foundations, ultimately anchored to the bedrock. It was dangerous work. Washington Roebling

Early photos of the bridge promenade. Note the Bridge Patrolman in the top photo.

personally supervised the workers until he contracted caisson disease, or the bends, and then oversaw construction from his home in Brooklyn Heights, relaying commands via Morse code to his wife, Emily, who herself had studied advanced mathematics and bridge engineering.

Within five years, the tower foundations and towers themselves were complete. The most difficult work was just beginning, as hundreds of miles of steel cables strong enough to support 160,000 pounds per square inch needed to be woven. After the last cable was positioned in 1878, a taxpayers' lawsuit, charging that the bridge was unsound, threatened the entire project. The case dragged on for several months, and Washington Roebling agreed to the addition of stiffening trusses. The last element, the roadway, was finally built from the foundations to the towers, supported by the cables, and the bridge opened to traffic on May 24, 1883.

The Brooklyn Bridge checks off several "first" and "only" boxes. It was the first major bridge to cross the East River; it's the only NYC bridge with masonry-clad towers made of limestone, granite and Rosendale cement, a more durable mortar produced in Ulster County, NY. Its successors, the Williamsburg, Manhattan and all other major bridges reveal their steel skeletons (though the George Washington Bridge was originally planned with brick coverings on its towers). For many years, it was also the only major NYC bridge featuring diagonal suspension cables, though in recent years the cable-stayed Kosciuszko and Goethals Bridges have employed diagonal cables.

The Manhattan skyline isn't the only available vista. Looking south across Upper New York Bay reveals Lady Liberty, the container vessel cranes on the Bayonne shore, and the Bayonne Bridge. At the two masonry towers, the walkways detour over the roadways and provide a look at the roadways beneath them. The bridge is not immune from graffiti that has to be scrubbed off from time to time. It had become a tradition for people to place padlocks on the cables to profess love and affection. Unfortunately, all that metal added weight to the bridge and risked destabilizing it, hence their removal. The bridge's cables and other aspects are constantly checked for safety. Shortly after the bridge opened in 1883, a rumor spread like wildfire among bridge walkers that it was collapsing, and the resulting stampede caused over a dozen deaths. No such collapse was happening, of course. [2]

The official invitation to the bridge opening

THE BROOKLYN BRIDGE POLICE DEPARTMENT

By section 8, chapter 300, Laws of 1875, the responsibility for policing the Brooklyn Bridge was given to the City of Brooklyn and New York City It was also made the duty of the trustees of the bridge to appoint an adequate police force and to regulate and direct the same for the protection of the bridge. The policemen so appointed would have and possess all the powers of policemen of the cities of New York and Brooklyn. [3]

There were 700 men employed on the bridge in one capacity or another and almost all were appointed by the president of the Bridge Trustees. The great majority of bridge employees owed their places to political influences. It was curious why there was never any legislation in Albany hostile to the bridge president and his administration, but this was easily explained by the judicious distribution of bridge patronage among the members of the legislature. There was hardly one of the 700 places on the bridge that was not looked upon as a choice job, much to be preferred above the general run of places in other employment. The positions on the bridge were considered even better than those of the same class in New York or Brooklyn.

As for the police jobs on the bridge, the Bridge Policemen thought their job was cleaner, softer, and easier on the feet. This was an interesting sentiment seeing as later I will talk about the extreme weather conditions as being one of the major complaints Bridge Policemen had regarding their working environment. Perhaps the positive feeling about working on the bridge had to do with feet. It had been noticed that the feet on the Bridge Policemen as a rule were not as large as those of the municipal police because a Bridge Policeman's foot did not swell much during the summer.[4]

Afterall, the condition of the feet was a huge issue for 19th century policemen. In fact, it was the origin of the term "flat foot," which alluded to the fact that police did so much walking on their beats that they developed the medical condition of flat feet. [5]

Initially officers were to be detailed from the existing police departments that covered the cities of New York and Brooklyn. Ultimately, the trustees of the bridge company gained total control over the newly created force.

Although the job may have been looked on positively, it did not seem that the cream of the crop wase brought on board to police the bridge. The men

The New York and Brooklyn terminals of the bridge.

selected by the trustees were below the standard of their counterparts in the cities and officers of the cities' police departments and the public were critical of the force from its inception. The force had a reputation as being a band of ruffians, with disproportionate levels of discipline and criminal complaints. Tammany Hall's political influence governed the force and Tammany intervened in the outcomes of disciplinary and criminal cases against bridge officers.

The bridge officially opened on Thursday, May 24, 1883. Traffic during the first weekend was very heavy, as sightseers flocked to enjoy the novelty of strolling hundreds of feet above the East River. Some thought the magnificent structure to be the eighth wonder of the world. According to the *New-York Tribune* the cities of New York and Brooklyn both wanted to make the opening of the bridge that would unite them a jubilant event. Flags, decorations and displays appeared on both sides of the river. A jeweler in Brooklyn formed a large model of the bridge out of his brightest gems. For the city of Brooklyn, it was a universal holiday. Seven thousand tickets let lucky persons onto the bridge on opening day. An additional six thousand or so held invitations to the opening ceremonies as well. Following military processions on both sides of the East River and gun salutes, dignitaries and guests met at the Brooklyn Terminal. Ceremonies began at two o' clock. After an opening prayer by the right Reverend Bishop Littlejohn, William C. Kingsley, of the Board of Trustees, formally presented the bridge to the mayors of the two cities.

Six ships of the U. S. Navy's North Atlantic Squadron were anchored under the bridge for the celebration. Chartered excursion boats, packed ferry boats and private yachts also took advantage of the river to view the bridge events. Later that day there were two regimental band concerts and another in the evening. Beginning at eight o' clock, fireworks were launched from the center of the bridge and also from both bridge towers. Over 14 tons were used during the hour-long display. Buildings in both cities were illuminated as part of the celebration. President Chester Arthur, the Governor and Mayor Low later attended a reception held at the Brooklyn Academy of Music

In the evening the bridge was opened to the public for a fare of one cent. In total, 150,300 people walked the bridge that day. Public excitement was immense, and the affair was not to be forgotten by those who were there. David McCullough in his book The Great Bridge wrote of this when he quoted a woman as saying the excitement over astronauts walking on the moon was nothing compared to what she had seen on the day they opened the Brooklyn Bridge. [6]

A Bridge Policeman patrols the promenade.

The bridge traffic settled down after the first three days. A big crowd was expected for Decoration Day, but provisions had been made the prevent any crush or jam. The Chief Engineer and Superintendent, C.C. Martin, was made the chief executive officer of the police force and said a force of twenty men was sufficient to handle the policing of the bridge. They would be on the lookout for issues specific to the bridge like throwing stones at the boats or streets below. Martin said with pride that in the crowded opening days there had not been one arrest for disorderly conduct.

The Bridge Police force was divided into two detachments of ten men, and they relieved each other every twelve hours. They were issued rattan canes for day work and regular police clubs for night. The entire force had new blue uniforms and James Ward, and ex-sergeant formerly of the 6th Precinct, was appointed Captain of the Bridge Police. [7] All orders were to be issued by Superintendent Martin in writing. In case of sickness or disability of the superintendent the captain would assume command.

Superintendent Martin took criticism for appointing Captain Ward. Ward was an ex-Sergeant of the Brooklyn Police Department and was recently demoted from the rank of Sergeant to Patrolman for incompetence. Ward resigned from the Brooklyn Police Department rather than accept the demotion. Brooklyn Mayor Seth Low told the trustees that the appointment of Captain Ward was "an unfortunate one."

The office of the Bridge Trustees was located on the Brooklyn side of the bridge at 22 Sands Street. The Bridge Police occupied some of the first floor and the basement with Captain Ward having an office in the basement.

The entire Bridge Police force was on duty on opening day. Their number of twenty-two officers was lost among the two hundred Brooklyn policemen under the command of Captain Alexander Williams and the five hundred officers from the New York Police Department under Inspector Murray on duty at the bridge for the opening ceremonies. [8]

Even a small fraction of these policemen would have been a Godsend less than a week later. The New York Tribune, on Monday, May 28, 1883, printed a front-page story indicating that in the few days it had been open the bridge might

Bridge railcars and the promenade.

C.C. Martin was the first Chief Engineer and Superintendent of the bridge making him, in essence, the Chief of the Brooklyn Bridge Police Department.

Captain James Ward was the highest-ranking uniformed
member of the Brooklyn Bridge Police Department.

have become too popular. It ominously mentioned that bridge workers, at one point on Sunday afternoon, feared a riot. Those fears became reality when the walkway of the Brooklyn Bridge[1] was the site of a shocking disaster on May 30, 1883, only a week after it opened to the public.

Decoration Day, the precursor to Memorial Day was being celebrated in the city. After morning rain, the day turned very pleasant. The New York Sun, on the front page of the next day's edition, described the scene:

"When the rain was over yesterday afternoon the Brooklyn Bridge, which had its crowds in the morning, but had become comparatively open again, began to threaten a blockade. With the hundreds who came downtown to the New York gates were hundreds of men in the uniform of the Grand Army of the Republic. Most of the people strolled over to Brooklyn, and then turned back without leaving the bridge. Thousands were coming over from Brooklyn, returning from cemeteries where soldier's graves had been decorated, or taking advantage of the holiday to see the bridge.

"There were not so many on the bridge as on the day after the opening, or on the following Sunday, but they seemed inclined to loiter. There would be an open space of from fifty to one hundred feet, and then a dense jam."

Problems became intense at the top of a nine-foot- high flight of stairs built into the walkway, near the point at which the main suspension cables passed by the promenade on the Manhattan side of the bridge. The pressing of the crowd pushed some people down the stairs. Somebody shouted out that there was danger, and the impression prevailed that the bridge was giving way beneath the crowd. The newspaper mentioned that a woman held her baby over the trestle work and begged someone to take it."

The situation had turned desperate. From the New York Sun:

"At last, with a single shriek that cut through the clamor of thousands of voices, a young girl lost her footing, and fell down the lower flight of steps. She lay for a moment, and then raised herself on her hands, and would have got up. But in another moment, she was buried under the bodies of others who fell over the steps after her. She was dead when they got her out more than half an hour afterward.

Men sprang upon the rails at the side and waved the crowds back from both the New York and Brooklyn sides. But the people continued to crowd on toward the steps. No police were in sight. Men in the crowd lifted their children above their

---

1.   https://www.thoughtco.com/building-the-brooklyn-bridge-1773695

heads to save them from the crush. People were still paying their pennies at both gates and swarming in."

Within minutes the frantic scene had calmed. Soldiers, who had been parading near the bridge in Decoration Day commemorations, rushed to the scene. The New York Sun described the aftermath:

"A company of the Twelfth New York Regiment worked hard at dragging them out. Twenty-five seemed to be nearly dead. They were laid along the north and south sides of the pathway, and the people from Brooklyn passed on between them. Men and women turned faint at the sight of the swollen and blood-stained faces of the dead. Four men, a lad, six women, and a girl of 15 were quite dead, or died in a few moments. They had been found at the bottom of the heap.

The police stopped grocers' wagons coming from Brooklyn, and, carrying the bodies of the wounded and climbing down the planks to the road, laid them in the wagons, and told the drivers to hurry to the Chambers Street Hospital. Six bodies were laid in one wagon. The drivers whipped up their horses and drove with full speed to the hospital."

Newspaper accounts of the dead and wounded were heartbreaking. The New York Sun described how one young couple's afternoon stroll on the bridge turned tragic:

"Sarah Hennessey was married on Easter and was walking on the bridge with her husband when the crowd closed in upon them. Her husband injured his left arm a week ago and clung to his wife with his right hand. A little girl fell in front of him, and he was thrown upon his knees and kicked and bruised. Then his wife was torn from him, and he saw her trampled upon and killed. When he got off the bridge he searched for his wife and found her in the hospital."

Rumors of the disaster spread quickly through the city. The New York Tribune reported that an hour after the accident it was told in the vicinity of Madison Square that 25 persons were killed and hundreds wounded, and at 42nd Street that the bridge had fallen down and 1,500 had lost their lives.

Within just a few minutes the frenzy had passed, but twelve people had been crushed to death. Hundreds more were injured, many seriously. The deadly stampede placed a dark cloud over what had been a celebratory first week[2] for the bridge.

In the days and weeks following the disaster the blame for the tragedy was directed at the management of the bridge. Bridge officials were criticized for failing to place Bridge Policeman at strategic places to keep crowds dispersed. Subsequently, it became standard practice for uniformed officers on the bridge to keep people moving along, and the Decoration Day tragedy was never repeated.

The fear that the bridge was in danger of collapsing was, of course, completely unfounded. The Brooklyn Bridge has been renovated to some extent, and the original trolley track was removed in the late 1940s and the roadways changed to accommodate more automobiles. But the walkway still stretches down the middle of the bridge and is still in use. The bridge is crossed every day by thousands of pedestrians, and the promenade with striking views that drew revelers in May 1883 is still an attraction for tourists today. [9]

Shortly after the disaster there was an inquest conducted where there was testimony regarding the causes of the tragedy. There was some testimony condemning the Bridge Police and other statements acquitted them of responsibility. One testifier alleged that the bridge was improperly policed that day because the policemen assigned to the bridge received a salary of only two dollars a day. That allegation was quickly countered by pointing out that if the testimony was accurate, the accident would not have happened if the policemen's salaries had been raised the day before the accident. The testimony seeking to condemn the police continued by saying that the policemen were not experienced, not properly trained, and not in uniform.

I found that last statement very interesting. It is the only reference I could find indicating that the Bridge Policemen were not in uniform during the early days after the bridge opened.

The counter argument to the policemen being inexperienced and untrained was that they were led by a very experienced policeman in Captain Ward. In a very unique attempt to counter the claim of inexperience it was pointed out that many of the policemen were formerly employed as riggers during the construction of the bridge. They would be able to learn the police trade quickly, but their prior employment gave them the distinct advantage of being able to climb about the trestle work to handle any dangerous situation. Operationally, there was testimony stating that even though their uniforms were not ready, the policemen did have

Bridge railcar station and early view of bridge.

their badges and twenty-two of them were on duty at the time of the disaster. This is an interesting contradiction because in every other article I researched, the initial number of men in the department was listed as twenty.

The testimony indicated that the policemen were distributed about the bridge and two were at each stairway. There had been testimony alleging that if more policemen had been stationed at the dangerous point of the disaster, it may have been averted. Other testimony, however, claimed that the presence of more policemen would have served to narrow the pathway even more, and that it would have required forty policemen working 12-hours a day each to police the stairways effectively. [10]

For his part Superintendent Martin believed that the Bridge Police performed well during the tragedy. He indicated that the police were abundantly able to handle much larger crowds than crossed the bridge on Decoration Day. He did concede that it was possible that policemen who had been well-drilled in crowd control might have helped to avert the panic. Martin went on to say that once the panic started, however, there was no way to stop it. Martin admitted that he considered the iron railings that had been erected at the center of the stairways a source of danger, explaining that while one side of the stairway was almost empty the other side was completely jammed. He suggested that policemen stationed at the stairs would be far more valuable that any iron railings. [11] Two months after the tragedy Captain Ward said he believed the Bridge Police force was now well organized and in better working order than any body of police in Brooklyn or New York. [12]

The trustees of the Brooklyn Bridge held a meeting to go over precautions necessary to prevent future accidents. It was decided that additional policemen were necessary, and Superintendent Martin was authorized to employ them. The police departments of Brooklyn and New York were to cooperate in furnishing police when necessary. The force would be tripled bringing the manpower to 66 men, and the hours would be reduced from 12 to 8. At least twenty policemen would be on duty at all times. Telephone connection to both sides of the bridge would be pushed rapidly, and policemen were stationed at the stairs and narrow portions of the promenade. No one was allowed to loiter at these points. [13]

One of the catalysts to the panic on the bridge was when someone yelled out that the bridge was collapsing. It may seem ludicrous now that such an assertion could stir panic, but at that time predictions of the Brooklyn Bridge's collapse had been common. In 1876, at about the halfway point of its construction, the chief mechanic of the bridge crossed between the Brooklyn and Manhattan towers on a cable to publicly demonstrate confidence in the bridge's design.

Earlier in 1883, another method to instill public confidence in the bridge had been suggested. Showman and circus founder P.T. Barnum had suggested marching his elephants, led by his most famous one, Jumbo, across the bridge in celebration of its opening. He was turned down, but with public trust of the structure still wavering, a display of the Brooklyn Bridge's strength seemed to be a good idea. On May 17, 1884, Barnum marched twenty-one elephants across the bridge along with seventeen camels. The animals made it across just fine, proving that the bridge was steady. [14]

Captain Ward was to be held strictly responsible to the superintendent for the preservation of order and the public peace on the bridge and its approaches, and he was empowered to place the men under his command in such positions as he may deem expedient. In absence of the captain the senior roundsman would assume command. [15]

"Roundsman" may be an unfamiliar term to most people. In the 19th century a platoon of New York police was commanded by a sergeant and broken into sections under the supervision of a roundsman. The title for these first line supervisors was given because they made the rounds checking on the patrolmen but was abolished during the first decade of the 20th century. [16]

For the bridge opening, Superintendent Martin appointed twenty policemen at $2.00 a day. Originally, the policemen were divided into two platoons with each working 12 hours, but they were quickly changed to 8-hour shifts. I did find another huge contradiction in the original manpower of the bridge force. An 1896 news article stated that when the bridge opened in 1883 the police force had 104 men. The context of the story was that of the original 104 only 26 were remaining on the force in 1896. [17]

The article went on to say that from 1883-1896 fifty officers died and twenty-eight resigned or were dismissed. Of the men who died nearly all of them suffered from lung trouble or rheumatism owing to the dampness and drafts which were marked characteristics of the bridge. The article further noted that when they joined, they were all strong and healthy but gave way under the severe exposure. I'll speak more about the weather conditions on the bridge later. So, was the correct number 20 or 104 on the bridge for opening day? I tend to go with 20 as I'll explain when we look deeper into those first few weeks after the bridge opened. [18]

After the bridge tragedy the initial reaction was to greatly increase the number of Bridge Policemen. The further the tragedy faded into the past, however, the more the trustees talked about reducing the size of the force. Captain Ward argued to maintain a certain staffing level of the Bridge Police force with rationale that was unique to the time period. He noted that a policeman had limited visibility at night and how easy it would be if there were less policemen for someone to throw a person off the bridge without being detected.

The trustees argued that the captain could maintain the same police coverage with less men if they worked 12-hour shifts instead of 8-hours. Captain Ward said that 12-hour shifts would never work because it was dangerous. The men could not stand being on the bridge in very cold weather for 12-hours. He told the trustees that they had no idea how terrible the winter conditions on the bridge were. He also took a shot at the city police by commenting that the Bridge Policemen were exposed to the elements at all times and could not slip into a warm and friendly corner gin mill like the city policemen.

While explaining why the 12-hour tours would not work, Captain Ward laid out the typical deployment of the officers on the bridge. Captain Ward stated that there were about 80 men on the Bridge Police force divided into three platoons with each platoon working an 8-hour shift. He said that 26-men were assigned to each platoon, but he cautioned the trustees at considering that number because he pointed out that there were always men excused due to sickness or other reasons.

There was one policeman posted in the south roadway at the Brooklyn entrance to keep vehicles from being driven off the bridge at full speed and to prevent people from entering the bridge in the wrong lane. Policeman #2 was posted at the exit foot of the railroad stairs to prevent people from entering without paying. Policeman #3 was at the penny toll-box to regulate the travel there. Policeman #4 was posted at the entrance to the north roadway to take care of the vehicle travel on that side. Policemen #5 and #6 were on each station platform. In the evenings and mornings when there was a rush, four men were required on the platforms, one to look after each car gate and prevent people from crowding over each other and getting on the cars when they were in motion. Policeman #7 stood at the upper end of the exit to keep people from coming back and blocking up the toll box. The same number of men were required on the New York side making the amount of posted police fourteen.

Captain Ward continued that two patrolmen were placed on each roadway to prevent fast driving and to keep vehicles to the right so that there would be no collisions. One man patrolled from the station up to the steps of the Brooklyn tower. Ward pointed out that this post could not be eliminated because the policemen stood on each tower to attend to the telephone, to keep people from sleeping on the benches, to assist those suddenly taken ill, and to prevent improper conduct. There were also two patrolmen patrolling between the towers. Captain Ward said that instead of looking to reduce the force the trustees should be looking to increase the manpower because there should be more patrolmen posted on the roadways. He pointed out how reckless some drivers on the bridge were and how many of them drove slowly until they passed the policeman.

Captain Ward said that the Bridge Police force had kept the bridge safe since it opened, but that if criminals became aware of less police protecting the bridge, they would quickly make it their hunting ground, emphasizing that bunko steerers, loose and improper characters, thieves and blackmailers would quickly make the bridge their home. [19]

I found a manpower breakdown several times throughout the brief history of the department. The report of the Bridge Police Department for the year 1886 showed that the force consisted of 97-men, 18 of whom were hired during the year. [20]

In 1889 there was 1 captain 1 sergeant 3 roundsman 1 property clerk and 92 policemen. [21]

1894 was a year of big changes for the Bridge Police Department. The Governor approved a bill giving the Brooklyn Bridge Police parity with Brooklyn Police. The force manpower broke down as follows:

1 captain – James Ward

2 sergeants – Edward F. Phillips and William J. Hayes

3 roundsmen

84 patrolmen

90 in total on force [22]

In 1895 the force numbered 84 patrolmen, 3 roundsmen, 2 sergeants, and 1 captain. [23]

One of the main roles of the Bridge Police was to make sure tolls were paid – penny for pedestrian and 10 or 30 cents for drivers. Superintendent Martin pointed out that the bridge was constructed to provide sure and rapid communications between the two cities. and was not a place where leisure hours were to be spent and from which sights could be seen. He conceded that there was no better vantage point to view the city, and that pedestrians were welcome to enjoy the view so long as they did not interfere with the flow of traffic. But he stressed that the interests of business took priority, so he wanted the police to concentrate on maintaining the bridge rules that kept traffic flowing. There was one promenade and pedestrian volume could become dangerous, so pedestrians were required to keep to the right with those wishing to move slowly and look at the scenery staying near the railing. The same plan was adopted on the two roadways. New York bound vehicles used the road on the right side of the bridge with heavily laden and slow-moving teams on the right side of the road and light wagons and carriages nearest the center. [24]

In 1889 the Bridge Police were granted a pay increase to $1,050.00 a year, but the increase was offset by a new regulation requiring the policemen to pay for their own uniforms. Previously, the uniforms were supplied to the policemen.

The five required uniform garments cost $68.50 new and $40.75 a year to maintain. Eventually, the trustees rescinded the requirement for policemen to purchase their own uniforms with pay fixed at 34.5 cents per hour with bridge trustees furnishing the uniform.

A dress coat was adopted, and the president was authorized to obtain bids for a completely new uniform. Gray uniforms had been contemplated but the idea was received very unfavorably by the men.

The trustees met to accept the sealed bids for supplying uniforms for the Bridge Police. The problem was that the president had already awarded the contract to Charles E. Teale & Company. When the bids were opened B. Stern & Son was the lowest bidder.

Bridge President James Howell said there was no time because he wanted the new uniforms to be ready in time for the Centennial celebration. [25]

The Centennial occurred in 1889 and celebrated the inauguration of George Washington one hundred years earlier. It was a huge event in New York City with three days of parades, fireworks, receptions, and concerts. [26]

General Barnes, one of the trustees, mentioned that they had already ordered uniforms and that the committee authorized President Howell to order the uniforms so the police could present a desirable look in new dress uniforms for the Centenary.

Mayor Grant wanted to know why the bids were not advertised and Howell said there was no time. The mayor was angry, pointing out that a resolution had been passed that bids must be solicited for all bridge supplies – including uniforms

General Barnes was good natured saying that he was so concerned with having the policemen look good for the Centenary he forgot about the resolution. [27]

At first it was suggested that the police salary should be increased by $50 dollars a year and allow them to purchase their own uniforms. This was an attempt to let Teale keep the business by having the policemen continue to utilize them with their own money. The contract was eventually awarded to Stern but with the stipulation that they take Teale's partly finished uniforms, and the trustees would pay Teale for the work they already completed. [28]

Chief Martin also notified that the bridge would continue to furnish uniforms, but the police would now have to pay for them, and the cost would begin being deducted from their pay in installments in their June July and August salaries. Some policemen threated to get lawyer to fight this. [29]

Bridge patrolmen wore shields, which were inscribed "New York and Brooklyn Bridge Police." In 1885 they received new badges. The old ones were worn out and disreputable looking. They were made by a man who designed baggage checks and were not pretty to start with. The new badges bore a representation of the bridge on their nickel-plated faces and were altogether handsome. [30]

In 1894 the Bridge Police gained pay parity with the City of Brooklyn. When the new pay rate for Bridge Policemen went into effect, it should have been a happy moment for the force, but some policemen were not happy. In gaining parity with the Brooklyn force, they expected to be paid $1,100 a year, but Superintendent Martin said that since they received the same pay as the Brooklyn city police, they should also be placed in the same pay structure. Accordingly, those with one year received $800 – two years $900. Those with three or more years received $1100. Captain Ward was paid $2700 – sergeants Phillips and Hayes $1750 and the three roundsmen $1200

Parity also came with an additional price when the trustees decided that parity did not include only pay. They said that Bridge Policemen had to be held to the same physical standards as their Brooklyn counterparts. Therefore, it was necessary to have all members of the present bridge force receive a physical examination. The superintendent directed all members of the police force, including captain, sergeants, roundsmen and patrolmen to report to the surgeon of the trustees for physical examinations and that a report would go to the superintendent with the results of such examinations. The superintendent would then report to the executive committee the names of the policemen best qualified, in his judgement, mentally, morally, and physically, to constitute the police force of the New York and Brooklyn Bridge. [31]

When the smoke cleared in 1894 the Bridge Police had equality with Brooklyn in all matters except pension. [32]

Here are some of the specific rules for Bridge Police, as written at the time. THE RULES FOR PATROLMEN

Rule No. 1 – Every member of the force when entering on duty must be neat in his person, his clothes and shoes clean, and his dress in conformity with the regulations prescribed by the superintendent.

Rule No. 2 -Every member in his conduct and deportment must be quiet, civil, and orderly. In the performance of his duty, he must maintain decorum and attention, command of temper and patience; must be discreet and use good judgement. He must at all times refrain from harsh, violent, course, profane or insolent language, and when required, act with firmness and sufficient energy and force to perform his duty.

Rule No. 3 - Punctual attendance, prompt obedience of orders and conformity to the rules will be rigidly enforced.

Rule No. 4 – He will not leave his post until regularly relieved; leaning, lounging, slouching attitudes, swinging and rolling movements are strictly forbidden.

Rule No. 5 – He shall not use his club except in urgent cases.

Rule No. 6 – Every member of the force must recollect that in making an arrest he is not justified in doing more than is absolutely necessary for the safe custody of the prisoners until he conveys them to their proper destination. It is the duty of a bridge policeman to keep his prisoners safely, but he has no right to use unnecessary violence, and he must not use such language as would be calculated to provoke or exasperate them, for such conduct tends to create resistance and a hostile feeling among the bystanders toward the policemen.

Rule No. 7 – The bridge policemen should not become offended at any harsh or abusive language that may be applied to them.

Rule No. 8 - Each member shall at all times have with him a small book in which he will enter the names of persons taken in charge by him, the names of witnesses and such particulars in each case as will be important on the trial of the case.

Rule No. 9 – Each member of the force shall devote his whole time and attention to his duties as a bridge policeman and he is expressly prohibited from following any other calling or being employed in any other business. Although certain hours are allotted to the respective roundsmen and patrolmen for the performance of duty on ordinary occasions, yet at all times they must be prepared to act immediately on notice that their services are required.

Rule No. 10 - Patrolmen must not walk together or talk with each other when they meet on the confines of their post unless to communicate information pertaining to their police duties, and in such case they must make the communication as brief as possible, and they must not engage in conversation with any person while on post, excepting in regards to matters concerning the immediate discharge of their duties.

Rule No. 11 – It shall be deemed a neglect of duty on the part of the patrolman to carelessly lose his badge, or to neglect to fasten it securely to his person, or to neglect to report the loss immediately after its occurrence to the officer in command.

Rule No. 12 – If he observes on the bridge anything to occasion damage or public inconvenience, anything that seems irregular, offensive or dangerous, measures must be taken to guard passengers from injury therefrom, and immediately report the same to his superior officer

These photos of Brooklyn Bridge Police Officers appeared in the Brooklyn Daily Eagle in 1942 under a segment called "Where are they now."

4 A   BROOKLYN EAGLE, SUNDAY, NOV. 22, 1942

Rule No. 13 – All lost property coming into the possession of any member of the force shall be delivered at the station house, with the particulars of the finding.

Rule No. 14 - He must, by his vigilance, render it extremely difficult, if not impossible, for anything of a serious nature to occur on his post without his immediate knowledge, and when on any post offenses frequently occur, there shall be good reason to suppose that there is negligence or want of ability on the part of the patrolman on the post.

Rule No. 15 – He shall strictly watch the conduct of all persons of known bad and of suspicious character, and in such a manner that it will be evident to such persons that they are watched, and that certain detection must follow the attempt to commit crime.

Rule No. 16 - Any member of the Bridge Police shall be dismissed from the force for any act of insubordination or disrespect toward his superior officer, for neglect of duty and for violation of the rules, for immoral conduct or conduct unbecoming an officer, or for any breach of the discipline of the force.

Rule No. 17 – It is forbidden to communicate except to such persons as directed by his superior officer, and information respecting orders he may have received, or any regulation that may be made for the government of force.

Rule No. 18 – The discreet exercise of the power of arrest is one of the most difficult of an officer's duties; in its performance, judgement, sagacity, skill and delicacy are demanded and must be observed, and in effecting an arrest no more force must be used than is absolutely necessary.

Rule No. 19 – All persons found intoxicated and disorderly, or committing or attempting to commit, an obscene or indecent act, must be promptly arrested. The police should be careful to discriminate between malicious offenses and those which are committed through thoughtlessness or ignorance, and act accordingly.

Rule No. 20 -They must give their names and numbers in a respectful manner to all persons who may ask for them.

Rule No. 21 – In all cases where one person charges another with a commission or attempted commission of an offense, and requests that the person charged be taken into custody, the officer shall require the person so complaining to accompany the prisoner and him to the station house, and there make a complaint in writing. In case the complainant refuses to do so, the officer will make no arrest.

Rule No. 22 – Any member of the force absent from duty or roll call without leave except in cases of sickness, will be liable to dismissal from the force, and the resignation of no member of the force will be accepted while a charge is pending against him. [33]

There was also a minimum weight requirement for members of the department

Weight requirements

Height Weight

5 7.5 133

5 8 135

5 9 140

5 10 145

5 11 150

6 155

6 1 160

6 2 165

6 3 170

6 4 175 [34]

POLICE WORK

So, what exactly did the bridge police do as it related to policework. They did the same thing all police officers do – they protected the people and property within their geographical area of employment. The unique aspect for this police department was that their geographical area of employment happened to be a bridge.

The annual report for 1886 prepared by Sergeant Phillips reflected the following activity:

Staffing: 97 men 18 of whom who had been appointed during the year.

331 arrests 243 of which have resulted in a sentence. The most frequent offenses involved intoxication and disorderly conduct.

96 simple intoxication cases

72 drunk and disorderly cases

68 fast drivers

34 runaways

3 attempted suicides

3 successfully jumped

16 ships have lost topmasts

39 accidental injuries [35]

In 1889 there were 191 arrests all of which were disposed of except for one case. Three persons died on the bridge and 72 persons were accidentally injured by falling on the stairs and platforms and from other causes. There were 36 runaways, 15 causing slight damage and 21 no damage. 35 persons were taken ill on the bridge and 8 lost children were found. Two vessels lost their topmasts when they struck the bridge. [36]

A word about "runaways." These were not children running away from home. These were horses pulling vehicles that began running amuck on the bridge. At least they were usually horses. Take for example, the experience of Bridge Officer Dooley, who was patrolling his beat near the New York entrance to the bridge. Early in the morning Dooley received a message by telephone from the Brooklyn side directing him to stop three runaways that were coming over the bridge. Dooley, expecting to see three frightened horses ran to the big gate and opened it. A wagon carrying produce came into view with the driver screaming to keep the gate open until he passed through. When the wagon passed through Dooley was able to close the gate in time to halt the three runaways – who were camels. They were in transit from Coney Island to Central Park and had broken away from their leaders, a man and two boys. Officer Dooley said the beasts were the wildest animals he had ever seen come over the bridge except for some wild revelers that cross almost nightly. [37]

Sometimes the horses weren't runaways, but still presented a police problem. Such was the case for Officer Shattuck who arrested a drunk who was driving a horse drawn wagon at the New York bridge entrance. Captain Ward checked the address on the wagon and found that the horse and wagon were stolen. [38]

Most of the cases handled by the Bridge Police were not as unusual as the camels, but there were other out of the ordinary incidents. There was a unique aided case where Henry Berg dislocated his thumb on the bridge and was taken to the Bridge Police station on Sands Street on the Brooklyn side. From there he was sent to Dr. J.J. Keane on Johnson Street who dressed it. Berg refused to pay the $3.00 charge, claiming it was exorbitant. The doctor then knocked Berg down and threw him out the door. Berg made a complaint at the 1st Precinct station house, but the doctor said it was Berg who started the fight. [39]

One of the less glamorous aspects of police work involves dealing with people under severe emotional stress. Most police departments refer to these individuals as emotionally disturbed persons, or EDPs. The Bridge Police handled their fair share of EDP's, but back in the 19th century they used other descriptive terms.

One morning officer Lally (remember that name) was on duty at the Brooklyn entrance when he noticed a man acting in a strange manner on Sands Street. When taken before Captain Ward the man said his name was Matthew Nelson and he was 31 years of age. He was unable to tell his residence and other circumstances showed he was suffering under a fit of insanity. Captain Ward sent him to the Commissioners of Charities Office. [40] Somehow, I don't think "fit of insanity" would be an acceptable way for a police officer to characterize an aided case today.

In another case, Officer Hill of the Bridge Police saw a man climbing from the footpath over the railroad track at 8;30 pm. He asked him what he was doing, and the man responded, "nothing." The policeman thought he might jump and took him to the station house on the Brooklyn side. Police said

Jensen, a 31-year-old printer had the bugs, or delirium tremors. [41] I don't think "bugs" was any better than "fit of insanity."

Sometimes, the Bridge Police actually dealt with real crimes. As William Arnold, a printer, ascended the steps to the Brooklyn Bridge one night he was tripped by John A. Williams, also a printer. At the same moment Williams snatched Arnold's watch and darted up the roadway. Officer Lanny, of the Bridge Police captured Williams and locked him up in the Oak Street station house. [42]

The bridge was not immune to any crime, including fraud. There are two names that have contributed prominently to the lore of the Brooklyn Bridge – George C. Parker and Steven Brodie. What? You never heard of these gentlemen. We will talk about Mr. Brodie in a future chapter so let me start with Mr. Parker.

For as long as I can remember I have heard the phrase, "If you believe that, I have a bridge in Brooklyn to sell to you." The phrase originated because for over a century people have fallen for the con that New York City is selling the Brooklyn Bridge.

George C. Parker, a native New Yorker, was responsible for originating the phrase. Parker became famous for selling New York City landmarks of all kinds ranging from Madison Square Garden to the Statue of Liberty. He also sold the Metropolitan Museum of Art and even Grant's tomb as the general's grandson.

He would set up fake sales offices and forge documents to support his cons. One of his most popular places for spotting rubes or victims was Ellis Island where some of the immigrants came with money to invest in new enterprises. Out-of-town tourists on their first visit to New York comprised another favorite target.

His greatest con was selling the Brooklyn Bridge. Legend claimed that he sold it at least twice a week. He did sell it several times including at least once for $50,000! The new owner discover he was the victim of a con when the bridge police officers stopped the "new owner" from setting up toll booths in the middle of the bridge.

The Brooklyn Bridge had been a toll bridge that pedestrians had to pay a penny to cross when it opened for business in 1883. Tens of thousands crossed the bridge every day on the way to work from Brooklyn to Manhattan. When the Brooklyn Bridge first opened, it cost a penny to cross by foot, 5 cents for a horse and rider and 10 cents for a horse and wagon. Farm animals were allowed at a price of 5 cents per cow and 2 cents per sheep or hog. Under pressure from civic groups and commuters, the pedestrian toll was repealed in 1891. The roadway tolls were then rescinded on July 19, 1911, with the support of New York Mayor William J. Gaynor, who declared, "I see no more reason for toll gates on the bridges than for toll gates on Fifth Avenue or Broadway." One can imagine the shock to a new immigrant who looked forward to making a fortune in America by virtue of the tolls from his new bridge when the bridge policemen approached and shattered his dream.

At one point, George Parker earned the title as "the greatest con man" but he kept on getting caught. Finally, in 1928 upon his third conviction for conning people, Brooklyn Judge Alonzo G. McLaughlin sentenced him to mandatory life imprisonment to Sing Sing Prison, where he died. [43]

Most of the frauds were not as flamboyant as attempts to sell the bridge. A typical example was a series of complaints made about confidence men who haunted the neighborhood of the Brooklyn Bridge trying to lure new immigrants into gambling houses. As a detective stood behind a pillar of the elevated railroad, he saw men rush forward to a man who had just exited the bridge grasping his hand and claiming to know him. The man shook him off and the detective made an arrest. [44]

As with all police departments there were unfortunate incidents involving dogs. This report turned in by Bridge Officer Hackings said a lot about the officer's writing ability.

July 18, 1896 6:30 am – A small tramp dog came over the promenade this morning and on the river span he took a fit and wint mad the passengers were all feard off him so I had to kill him. Officer Hackings true him overboard. [45]

Another trait the Bridge Police shared with modern police was the desire to avoid paperwork, even if it meant failing to report an incident. There was a case of a train car reaching the Brooklyn side and slamming into another car at ten o'clock in the evening. A dozen passengers were thrown out of their seats and were frightened, but not hurt. A New York Times reporter met with misrepresentation and suspicion from police when inquiring about the incident. The reporter was assured there was no damage but when he went to the scene he saw that the platform and the cars were substantially damaged. He was then chased away by the police because no one but employees could be in the track area. The reporter also learned from an unknown source that the brakes weren't working, and the car was traveling too fast. The police made no report of the incident to the bridge police station on the Brooklyn side and the sergeant on duty said he knew nothing about the incident other than that there had been some type of collision. [46]

Overall, crowding and rowdyism were prime issues for the police on the bridge, and they received pressure in the media as illustrated by the following article.

In the old days of leisure and room and courtesy before we had tenements and unions and trolleys a woman would be sure of courteous treatment by any company of men. In Manhattan she is sure of discourteous treatment. Whether young or old, modest or brazen, whether she is an idler in society or a working girl, she is rushed and hustled and the seat she may have expected is occupied by an eager scamp who jams his elbow into her side, pushes her hat over her face and sometimes throws her down in his fear that she may reach the place before him. Then he complacently draws a yellow paper out of his pocket and reads or pretends to, while the car goes inching along the slow, cold unpleasant journey across the bridge. We are not proud of this phase of city life. We are far from proud of the bullies and hobble-de-boys who commit virtual assault and battery on the weaker and older passengers and who seem to have less and less regard for the decencies and amenities of life as time goes on. But in general behoof we must maintain these decencies. We cannot actually take one of these stout young villains by the collar and trousers and fling him through the window though it would be a joy to do it. He really has a right to a seat for he has paid for it. But the kind of fellow who will possess himself of a seat while a tired working woman stands before him must at least be made to give that girl a chance to enter the car without bodily danger. He must be checked in his fierce scramble and arrested if he persists in punching and elbowing. People, who by nature are ruffians, can be made by law, not gentlemen, but harmless citizens, and the bridge police must see that the strenuous and hoggish fellows behave themselves. [47]

One way the Bridge Police dealt with these conditions was to perform enforcement sweeps of "Climbers." Climbers were those passengers who just couldn't wait to enter a train car via the door and instead climbed through the window. In one such sweep the Bridge Police locked up fifty climbers, all of who received one dollar fines. A newspaper article describing the sweep noted that rowdyism was a menace and recommended the temperate use of the club in dealing with the rowdies. [48]

Winter on the bridge was a busy time for the Bridge Police. Looking out for people who had their ears and noses frozen was one of the chief duties. A man was not always conscious that his nose was freezing. Sometimes the police had to argue with a man that his chief facial ornament was in danger. The policemen were fast becoming expert nose doctors. A policemen noted on a particular frigid night that he had saved three noses and that all eight policemen on duty that night found at least one patient. [49]

During one 24-hour period forty people were frostbitten while crossing the bridge. In the majority of cases the Bridge Police cared for them in the waiting room by the application of water to the parts affected. Some were treated at the tower houses. One unfortunate was found near the Brooklyn tower by a squad of policemen who were crossing. He was unable to proceed further and would have frozen to death had he not been discovered. He was attired in very thin clothing. The police enveloped him in several rubber coats, placed a pair of gloves on his hands and then led him to the side. After recovering sufficiently to talk, he said he had just been released from Brooklyn prison where he had served three months. He was utterly destitute and had no home. A collection was taken up among the policemen and some ladies in the waiting room. At the Chambers Street Hospital about twenty men and boys were treated for frostbite of the ears, nose, hands, and feet. [50]

The Bridge Police also suffered from the effects of the weather. Patrolman John J. Smith resigned because he said he could not stand the exposure on the span and said his life was more valuable to him than his position. Smith has been on the bridge police force for five years and his post had been on the river span, where he was constantly exposed to the cold winds of the winter and the heat of the summer. He had a good record and had been complaining of not feeling well and had been on the sick list and under the doctor's care, all of which in his opinion was due to constant exposure on the bridge. [51]

As I conducted the research for this book, I found some interesting correlations between the Bridge Police and the New York City Transit Police Department I had been a part of. Despite being full-service police officers, the upper management of the Transit Authority and Transit Police Department frowned on transit cops leaving the subway system to take police actions. I received the same vibe when reading about the bridge management. In a previous chapter where I was citing some of the rules bridge policemen worked under, it was noted that there was a rule prohibiting them from wearing their uniforms while off duty. It was further explained that the rationale for this rule was so that the public would not confuse bridge officers, who have jurisdiction only on the bridge, with regular police officers.

Apparently, the bridge officers were in the habit of wearing their uniforms to and from the bridge because they did not pay car fare while in uniform. I tend to believe the main reason for the prohibition of wearing uniforms while off duty was to discourage police action anywhere but on the bridge.

Police officer powers are granted statewide, and just because a police officer is not within his or her geographical area of employment doesn't mean they can't take a police action. For example, a member of the NYPD who observes a crime while off duty in upstate New York is still a police officer and may take police action. Therefore, I think bridge management may have been intentionally vague in stating that the bridge officers had no jurisdiction off the bridge. Certainly, the bridge was their geographical area of employment, but they were still full-service New York State empowered police officers with the authority to take police action off the bridge.

I do, however, understand the bridge management's point of view. If an officer made an arrest on the way to work on the bridge that would be one less post covered during that shift and whatever the arrest was for would not count as a statistic for the department because it did not occur on the bridge.

Sometimes, the Bridge Police couldn't help but take action off the bridge. Through their vigilance, even though they were not supposed to watch the New York docks, one of the most notorious gangs of thieves that infested the riverfront was brought to justice. Early one morning Officer Connell was working on the bridge when he noticed a boat containing two men passing back and forth between the Dover Street dock and a boat loaded with cotton on the Bridge Pier. He notified Sergeant Phillips who by telephone ordered officers O'Brien, English, and Fisher to investigate.

The gang had kept up the illegal activity because they believed the police were not sharp enough to catch them. The Bridge Police commented on the neglect of the New York Police in not following up the earlier thefts and finding a complainant as being neglectful and that the Bridge Police would not be able to regularly leave the bridge to do the work the New York authorities should be doing to catch the rest of the gang. [52]

Although the Bridge Police were not supposed to leave the bridge to take a police action, it was okay for them to take action on a crime that occurred off the bridge when it was reported on the bridge while the offender was on the bridge. For example, there was the case of James Leonard, a professional boarding house thief who was followed from a boarding house by a victim to the bridge entrance where he was arrested by Officer King. When he was taken to the Sands Street station a bridge employee recognized the coat he was wearing as one that was stolen from him weeks earlier. Leonard was tied to several other boarding house thefts and when he was searched, Captain Ward found 15 latch keys, all from boarding houses he had stayed at. [53]

New York City is no stranger to policing special events, and sometimes the Bridge Police were involved in events on the bridge.

Lieutenant Commander George Washington DeLong was born in New York City on 22 August 1844. He joined New York newspaper publisher James Gordon Bennett in planning an attempt to reach the North Pole in a ship specially strengthened to drift in the Arctic icepack.

Bennett purchased the British steam bark Pandora in 1878, renamed her Jeannette and turned her over to the U.S. Navy under the terms of a Congressional authorization to operate the ship, with Bennett bearing the costs. DeLong, who was to command the planned expedition, brought Jeannette from Europe to San Francisco, California, where she was refitted for ice navigation. In July 1879 he sailed for the Bering Strait, accompanied a crew of Navy officers and enlisted men plus a few civilian specialists. Jeannette entered the ice in early September and remained in its grip until June 1881, when she was broken open by its force and sank.

Lieutenant Commander DeLong then led his men on a heroic journey, of nearly three months duration, across the rugged ice to open water north of Siberia. There they launched the three boats that they had dragged along during their travels over the ice. One of the boats disappeared in a storm a few days later, its eight occupants becoming the expedition's first fatalities. The other two craft, including that commanded by DeLong, reached the Lena River Delta, where they landed at widely separated points. DeLong and his thirteen companions, suffering badly from frostbite, exhaustion and hunger, struggled southwards in an effort to find inhabitants. However, with exception of two men sent ahead to seek rescue, all died during October or the first few days of November 1881. The bodies of Lieutenant Commander George W. DeLong and nine of his men were discovered in March 1882 and, in early 1884, brought back to the United States for reburial. [54]

DeLong was buried in the Bronx, and when his remains were brought back to New York City the funeral procession proceeded from Brooklyn to the Bronx and crossed the Brooklyn Bridge. The procession as a big event in New York City with onlookers lining the route, including the bridge.

Commodore John Henry Upshur wrote a brief letter of thanks to the Bridge Police for their role in facilitating the DeLong procession.

From Commodore Upshur – Sincere thanks to the Bridge Police for their valuable service in the reception of the remains of the late Lt. Commander George W. De Long and his companions. Also, appreciation at not having to pay the toll.

I find it fascinating that the commander of the United States Navy's Pacific Squadron would thank the Bridge Police for letting the funeral procession of an American hero pass over the bridge without paying the toll. [55]

Have you ever lost something on a train or bus and wondered what happened to it? Most large transit systems have lost and found departments. The New York City Transit Authority has a huge lost and found operation with thousands of items coming into its possession each year. In the New York City system, recovered property is held for a certain period of time and if not claimed by the owner the property is either auctioned or, if it is in poor condition, sent for disposal.

When the Brooklyn Bridge opened, lost property was not a condition that was planned for, so when lost property began turning up in the train cars and on the promenade, the task of administering this found property fell on the Bridge Police.

The system which was adopted on the cars is as follows: A book was provided in which to keep a record of lost articles and each page consisted of a stub and three receipts. This book was kept at the Brooklyn police station. The conductors were all instructed that as soon as the passengers left the train to go through the car for lost articles and to deliver them at once to the trainmaster who wrote a description of items found on the stub of his book with the day, time, and the name of the conductor. The trainmaster made the same memorandum on each of the three receipts and gave it to the conductor. The other two with the article were sent to the police station in the basement at 33 Sands Street. One of the receipts was signed by the officer at the desk and returned to the trainmaster who placed it on file. The third receipt was retained at the station with the property. If the owner appeared to claim the property, he was required to sign the third receipt. During a nine-month period in 1884 215 items were found with 95 returned to owners. [56]

Even though the Bridge Police developed a system for recording found property, aside from an owner claiming the item, it appeared that disposal of the property was the only other method employed.

The Brooklyn Bridge was so popular with the public when it opened, the accumulation of so many disparate articles on the "cars" was likely a phenomenon that had not been planned for. As such, aside from owners appearing to claim their property, there was no program designed to locate the owners of the property on trains and streetcars. The simple solution utilized was to destroy the property.

Great assortments of odds and ends which had been picked up on the bridge cars and promenade were cremated in a big furnace. The collection would have made a wagon load. Included in one particular burn in 1885 was a hoop skirt which some lady had lost on the cars. There were twelve old hats of both sexes, baby clothes enough for a Mormon family, muffs and tippets and cuffs and collars, and lunch baskets and gripsacks, ten or twelve decrepit umbrellas, half a dozen pairs of glasses, a score of canes, several ladies' cloaks and gentlemen's overcoats, fifty or sixty parcels of old books and papers and general trash, workmen's tools of various kinds and an infinity of odds and ends."

Captain Ward was in charge of the disposal of the items. He commented that it gave him the cholera to look at it, but that it burned well. [57]

Sometimes valuable property was found on the bridge and returned to the owner – well, maybe not all the valuable property. S. Misrahi, a diamond dealer, called the Bridge Police station and claimed a small case containing chip diamonds which was found on the stairway of the Brooklyn terminal. Misrahi said that when he entered the terminal, he had a case in one of his outside coat pockets, and that the chip diamonds in the case at the time were worth about $375. Captain Ward said the case was found by a ticket chopper who turned it over to Bridge Patrolman Buckridge. Mr. Misrahi's joy turned to dismay when he was given diamonds worth about $50. The man who turned the case into the ticket chopper explained that he had found the diamonds on the stairway. He said that just before he picked up the diamonds, he saw a woman stoop down and gather up a handful of small diamonds. Misrahi lamented that the jewels carried off by the unknown woman were worth at least $320. [58]

New York City has always been a prime target for terrorism, especially in post September 11, 2001 era. To counter that threat the NYPD maintains a large Counterterrorism Bureau, and along with the FBI is an integral part of the New York Joint Terrorism Task Force. Back in 1898 there were no specialized anti-terrorism units in New York City, but the specter of terrorism was a viable threat.

The Spanish American War was underway, and the United States was engaged in combat in Cuba and the Philippines where those countries were fighting for independence from Spain. America's entry into the war caused fear that Spain would seek to strike a blow on U.S. soil. In New York City, the Brooklyn Bridge, as the only bridge in the city, stood out as a potential terrorist target. The New York City Police Department detailed officers to assist the Bridge Police in maintaining surveillance of the structure.

While talking about terror, let's not forget that police work also includes odd and funny incidents. There was a reign of terror for a short time in the bridge police station on the New York side on Washington Street at about seven o'clock in the evening when a small Scotch Terrier, apparently suffering from rabies, invaded the muster room. The first to make the discovery of the rabid dog was the station house pet, a black cat which had a three-week old kitten. With true feline instinct for her offspring the cat sprang on the dog's back and finally drove it out into the alley. In the meantime, there was a wild scramble of the station staff, who mounted chairs and tables to get out of the way while the fight was in progress. Patrolman Hoar finally ventured into the alley, and a well-directed shot from his revolver dispatched the animal. The name of the owner of the dog could not be learned but the cat was considered the heroine of the occasion. [59]

Walking on the bridge promenade during the Blizzard of 1888.

JUMPERS

"Because it's there" Those famous words were spoken by British climber George Mallory in 1924 when he was asked why he wanted to climb Mount Everest. In August of that year Mallory and his partner Andrew Irvine disappeared on the way to the summit. The large scope of public grief over their demise marked the beginning of Everest's allure and fascination. [60]

Long before Mallory uttered his famous words the daredevils and depressed of New York City flocked to the Brooklyn Bridge to jump because - it was there. It's difficult for people today to understand how wondrous the bridge was to the people of Manhattan and Brooklyn. Before the bridge opened the only way to venture from Brooklyn to Manhattan was by boat. Suddenly, the river could be traversed by a leisurely stroll that began in Brooklyn and terminated in Manhattan. The height of the bridge was an awesome sight to behold. Manhattan was not yet filled with skyscrapers, so the magnificent view provided from the promenade was enough alone to draw New Yorkers to the span, even if they weren't looking to move between cities. It was the height of the bridge, nearly 140 feet at center span, that brought another type of person to the bridge - the jumper. All police departments have crimes that are particularly sensitive to their environments, and for the Bridge Police, it was the person who sought fame or an end by hurling him or herself over the side.

Captain Ward realized very early the problem that would develop with jumpers, and it was one of the main reasons he gave Superintendent Martin for not reducing the Bridge Police manpower. Martin responded with a novel idea. He noted that at Niagara Falls the police did not attempt to stop fools who wanted to go over the falls in a barrel as long as they didn't cause a disturbance. He quoted an official as saying that as long as they behaved themselves, they could go over the falls on stilts. Martin said maybe they should follow the same practice at the bridge and simply let the people jump if that was their desire and a kind fate would kill off some of them. While many people have managed to jump off the bridge, the act was never authorized, even tacitly. Even with the prohibition, more than 1,300 suicides have occurred. There were ideas of creating a suicide barrier, but the idea wasn't realized because of engineering obstacles.

In 1885, Robert Odlum, the first known jumper, died as a result of his jump. Odlum, a 33-year old swimming instructor, made his attempt on May

19, 1885, just short of the second anniversary of the bridge opening. Up until the time of the fatal jump Odlum's highest jump had been 118 feet at the Genesee Falls, and it was Odlum's intention to eclipse the record as well as to gain notoriety to gain profitable engagements as a swimmer.

He also wanted to prove that people do not die by falling through the air. He reasoned that men and women would not hesitate to jump 100-feet from the roof of a burning building into a net if they read he had successfully jumped 140-feet from the Brooklyn Bridge.

Odlum had become something of a celebrity due to the water stunts he had attempted, some of which were with his friend, Paul Boyton.

He came to New York a week earlier and even though there was no mass media to publicize the event, the jump had been widely, if surreptitiously advertised to the point that many in the city were prepared to witness and celebrate the event. The Bridge Police were also aware of Odlum's intentions and were on guard to prevent the jump,

On the day of the jump the sporting and theatrical "in the know" crowd gathered in the "Ship," a west 29th Street saloon owned by Captain Paul Boyton. Among the interested parties in the saloon were heavyweight prizefighter Paddy Ryan, wrestler William Muldoon, as well as actors Henry E. Dixey, Eben Plympton, and Harry Lacey. Also present were an assortment of local gambling characters.

Odlum said he never felt better and feared only interference from the Bridge Police. "It is my business and not that of the police," were his parting words.

After leaving Boyton's saloon Odlum proceeded to Paddy Ryan's saloon near the bridge entrance on Broadway to wait for an opportune moment. Meanwhile, a chartered tugboat containing celebrities and other invited witnesses waited at the barge office.

The bridge police lay in wait to pounce on the jumper, so to outwit the police plan a friend of Odlum's took a cab across the bridge and was apprehended as the supposed bridge jumper. Odlum followed in a black covered wagon. "This is a bully joke on the police," he said as he stripped off his outer garments, and attired only in shirt and trunks, awaited the critical moment to leap.

He held his left arm rigidly down against his thigh and stretched his right hand at full length above his head with the palm open as a sort of rudder, intended to maintain his equilibrium

Robert Odlum — the first jumper from the
Brooklyn Bridge

Robert Odlum

The strong wind blowing at the time seemed to turn him slightly around. For a hundred feet he fell straight as an arrow, then he lost his balance and doubled up slightly and struck the water with his feet and right hip. The force of the blow seemed to twist his body double as he disappeared beneath the surface of the water.

Captain Boyton leaped overboard from the tug with his clothes on and reached Odlum, who was floating face down with his red shirt torn to bits by the force of the fall. When he was pulled aboard the tug Odlum murmured, "Is it over?" and "Did I make a good jump?"

The crowd of witnesses dispersed as the bridge police neared the scene leaving Odlum alone with Boyton and a few friends.

Odlum died before the ambulance arrived. James Haggart, the decoy, had been arrested by the Bridge Police and locked up on the Brooklyn side, but he was released when no valid charge could be found to hold him on. [61]

One year after Odlum's death, Steve Brodie claimed to be the first man to jump off the Brooklyn Bridge and survive. There were no witnesses and Brodie was accused of faking the jump by throwing a dummy from the bridge. The alleged jump happened on July 23, 1886. One month later Larry Donovan made the plunge into the waters of the East River, becoming the first confirmed survivor of the Brooklyn Bridge leap. [62]

The first claim by anyone to have jumped, and survived, from the bridge belonged to Steve Brodie, of Manhattan, who claimed that on July 23, 1886 he jumped from a height of 135 feet. Brodie's claims were supported by only two friends who claimed that they were in a boat on the East River awaiting

On July 23, 1886 witnesses saw what appeared to be a human figure plummeting from the Brooklyn Bridge into the East River. Several minutes later Brodie was dragged from the water by a boatload of his associates. Loudly, he claimed to have just leaped from the bridge and repeated his assertion upon reaching the shore. After hearing the claim, the Bridge Police promptly arrested Brodie. However suspicious the circumstances were, no one in the press seemed to care as they bought into Brodie's leap.

But did Brodie really jump? The newspaper accounts detailed everything they could about the jump, especially Brodie's motive, which was simple. He was

Steve Brodie

looking to make some money. He arranged with some friends who were to row out to the bridge and pick him up after the leap. Then he hitched a ride on a wagon and took the 135 feet plunge into the waters of the East River. No one, other than his friends, claimed to have seen him jump but they reported that he landed feet first with only minor bruises. His friends pulled him into the boat, rowed him back to shore, and proceeded to have a celebration during which Brodie was arrested.

Once out of jail he told his story to anyone who would listen and turned himself into a local celebrity. Such a celebrity that "doing a Brodie" meant doing something outrageous. But it could also mean throwing a dummy off the bridge and lying about it as later claims against him stated.

If fame and money was the motive, Brodie was successful. Regardless of it being fact or fiction, Brodie opened a tavern at 114 Bowery at Grand Street. It celebrated Brodie's stunt with an oil painting and a signed affidavit from the people who pulled him from the waters, which, mind you, were his friends. The saloon became a very popular hotspot in the city for many years. [63]

When eating at a Brooklyn club in 1930, Boxing Commissioner William Muldoon, who had been a witness to the Odlum leap, said of Brodie, "He was fished out of the river soaking wet, but if he leaped out of anything but the deck of a canal boat or a tug I will eat my hat instead of this fine meal." [64]

James Lunny a retired member of the Bridge Police force in 1930 supported William Muldoon in contending that Brodie never jumped. Lunny spent 16 years on the bridge and was on the south roadway that day but not near the center of the bridge. He said that nothing else was talked about among the policemen for a long time and not one said they saw him jump. [65]

A friend of New York City Police Sergeant Thomas Hastings had said that Hastings had actually witnessed Brodie jump. Many years later Hastings said that he had not seen Brodie jump because he was nowhere near the bridge when the event supposedly occurred. Hastings confirmed that he knew Brodie very well because he was a roundsman at the old Mulberry Street station house which was only a few blocks away from Brodie's saloon on the Bowery. Hastings said that one day he came right out and asked if he had jumped off the bridge to which Brodie responded that he had not and had never said he did. Hastings went on to say that Brodie would never talk about the jump to him again. [66]

Steve Brodie's Saloon
FINE CLOTHING
BRODIE
LAGER BEER

ON THE BOWERY
STEVE BRODIE
CHAMPION BRIDGE-JUMPER OF THE WORLD

Robert Odlum and Steve Brodie may well have gained the most notoriety, but jumpers continued to be a regular part of a Bridge Policeman's job. Lawrence M. Donovan, a 24-year-old printer employed by the *Police Gazette*, a periodical relating to police news became the first conformed jumper to survive.

Clara McArthur became the first woman to jump from the bridge, and it took her two tries. A newspaper article described McArthur as one of the new breed of women willing to try almost anything. In this case, however, her attempt of the daring feet was thwarted by the Bridge Police.

Captain Ward received a tip that a woman was going to jump, so he dispatched Sergeant Hayes and a squad of four patrolmen to proceed to the New York end and Roundsman Wiggins with four officers to the Brooklyn end. Shortly after 5 pm a carriage entered the New York side. Along with the driver was a pale faced man, a 27-year-old woman and a young child. The police contingent paid special attention to the carriage until it exited on the Brooklyn side. Shortly thereafter the same carriage made the return trip to New York, but this time the driver was the only occupant of the carriage. It turned out that the woman in the carriage had been Clara McArthur, who was accompanied by her pale faced husband and 5-year-old daughter. As evidenced by the boat in the water and the spectators lining the shore, McArthur had every intention of jumping, but had been scared away by the police presence. [67]

Captain Ward received no further tips and ten days later at 3:30 am Clara McArthur dropped off the bridge quietly in the darkness. She was taken to the Hudson Street Hospital as prisoner, charged with attempted suicide. Although when she was picked up, she was unconscious, she recovered several hours later.

McArthur was motivated by her wish to earn a living for her husband who was a railroad man out of work, and her five-year-old child. She had been told how easily she could earn $100 a week by jumping from the bridge, and afterward appearing in a dime museum. "It was not my fault," Mr. McArthur said in denying any responsibility for his wife's action. "My wife has a talent for bridge-jumping. She has not had any actual experience, but she has the right idea." [68]

Not all bridge jumpers gained the notoriety of Odlum, Brodies, Donovan and McArthur, but for the average Bridge Policeman jumpers were a normal part of the job.

A man was on a truck acting suspiciously when the driver nodded to Policeman Ludgate who followed, and when the man got off the policeman told him to return to the wagon or he would arrest him. A few minutes later the man thought the officer was not looking and got off again. He was climbing the railing of the bridge when the policeman took him to the bridge police station on the Brooklyn side. James Lee, 41 said he was merely riding in the truck and had no idea of jumping into the river. While in jail Lee told a Times reporter that he would try it again as soon as he got out. "Me and that bridge are bound to get acquainted," he said with great earnestness. "I have been a swimmer all my life. When I was a boy in the fourth ward, where my Uncle Maguire was a policeman, I dived head-first from the mast of the Great Republic and afterward from the crosstrees of the Great Eastern. I intended to make a flying head-first leap from the bridge and shall do it yet or someone will get a bullet through his head." [69]

Military personnel were also drawn to the bridge. The New York Times told of one of Uncle Sam's sailor boys, who in 1893, full of Bowery beer, tried to commit suicide by jumping from the Brooklyn Bridge. He was standing on the cable, waiting for a boat to pass, when he was caught by one of the Bridge Police. The name of the 26-year-old despondent Jack Tar was Max Koch, attached to the receiving ship Vermont. Several days earlier Koch secured a leave of absence and went on a spree, overstaying his leave and meeting with a variety of adventures. Early in the morning he started over the bridge from the New York end. When half-way across he sat on a bench and waited until Policeman Ludgate's back was turned. Then he scaled the iron framework over the bridge railway and ran across it on a plank and jumped to the carriageway. He was seen by the brakeman of a train who yelled to Policeman Ludgate, and the officer started in pursuit. Not being as nimble as the sailor, the officer was a minute or more in scaling the framework and crossing the plank, and when he reached the roadway the sailor, who had removed his shoes, was poised on the outer cable with his hands over his head ready to dive but waiting for a boat to clear the way below. The policeman grabbed Koch around the waist, hauled him down, and took him to the bridge police station in Brooklyn. There the man said that he was bent on killing himself and would jump from the bridge if it took till Christmas. [70]

Steve Brodie wasn't the only questionable jump. Harry Menier, 25, claimed to have leaped early in the morning with a parachute from the middle of the bridge into the river. Captain Ward, however, said the claim had no foundation.

Menier claimed to have been accompanied to the center of the bridge by Charles Lestrange, an aeronaut, who handed the parachute to him. The thrilling adventure was said to have happened at 6:25 am when there were few witnesses. Captain Ward questioned all the police on the bridge, but no one saw the event. [71]

This next jumping incident forced me to find the meaning or "cornetist," which turned out to mean a musician who plays a trumpet or cornet. Patrick Daley, a cornetist for 18 years was arrested for trying to jump off the bridge. The unhappy man said he always wanted to see the exact spot where that curious fellow Odlum leaped into the river. He said he made two previous visits to the bridge to find the truth, but the police wouldn't give any information. This time he was determined to make a personal investigation, so he took a ride on a truck to the middle of the bridge. When he got off the truck, he was observing the plank flooring when Policeman Kenny came along and for some reason dragged him off to jail. He tried to explain that he would never want to jump from such a height and on such hot day. He explained that he had enough problems of his own without trying to imitate Odlum, saying that he was not a fool and that bridge jumping had no attraction to him.

Officer John Kenny gave a different version. He said he was standing by the tower on the Brooklyn side when he saw people running toward the center of the span. He saw Daly climbing over the railing near the spot where Odlum jumped. Kenny said Daly was getting ready to jump when he grabbed him. Daly said he was going to jump and asked the officer to let him go down. On the way to the police station Daley then changed his version saying that he only wanted to make an estimate of the distance Odlum jumped, and that he was no crank. [72]

Sometimes the jump or claim of jump involved a mystery. Such was the case in a story detailed by the Times in 1900. On this particular night the Brooklyn Bridge Police wore a tired look and perspired as they tried to unravel a mystery – the second mystery in two days.

It started when a Brooklyn attorney claimed he saw someone jump from the north roadway of the bridge. The conductor on the train also saw a group of people gazing over the railing of the north roadway. That was usually a sign that someone had jumped so he stopped his car and got the attention of Policeman Blake who was standing on the south Roadway. Blake telephoned Sgt. Brophy at the Brooklyn side station

"Another one, eh," said Brophy. "Say, Blake, run down to the waterfront and see if he's come up yet."

Blake hurried down to the riverfront. At the foot of Dock Street, he saw two boys in a rowboat out in the river. They were hauling into the boat what appeared to Blake to be a man. Blake believed that the boys had been waiting in the boat for the jumper.

"Hey, you," yelled Blake to the boys, "bring that man in here."

The boys looked very much alarmed and confirmed Blake's suspicion that the jumper was in the boat. The boys rowed slowly and reluctantly to the dock.

"I went in with my pants on," whimpered the one who had been dragged out of the water.

"It makes no difference whether you jumped with your pants on or not," said Blake. "Put your clothes on and come with me." The scared boys went with the policeman to the station.

"Well, you got him quick enough," Sgt. Brophy remarked as the dripping boy entered.

"Ain't a feller gotter right ter go in if he's got his pants on?" sniveled the wet lad.

"What did you jump for?" the sergeant asked.

"Jump? I didn't jump."

"Are you the boy who jumped from the bridge?"

"Jump from the bridge? I only went swimming wit me pants on."

The boy s said they hired a boat out of Wallabout Basin to go swimming. They did say they saw something that may have been a body floating in the river.

Terry the attorney said he was crossing in a car and saw someone run across the roadway and disappear near the railing. Further investigation revealed that the car before Terry's had stalled and what Terry and the conductor may have seen were passengers who had gotten out of the car while waiting for the car to be repaired. The police accepted the explanation, but all officers were told to be on the lookout for a floating body.

A body was discovered the next day floating in the river near Williamsburg. I love the description that appeared in the Times article.

The man was about 45-years old, weighed 210 pounds, was 5 feet 10 inches in height, had brown eyes, good teeth, dark hair, and a sandy mustache. He wore a black mixed sack coat and vest, gray and black striped trousers, black satin necktie, blue and white striped outing shirt, balbriggan undershirt, black stockings and dark tanned shoes, size 9 bought from Joseph Loy of 11 Bond Street, Manhattan.

In his pockets were a small penknife, a single cuff button, a matchbox, a bunch of seven keys, two white handkerchiefs in a corner of one being the initial "S," a room check number 538 from Smith & McNells Hotel. There were also three $1 dollar bills. There were no marks visible on the body.

A man fitting the description had taken a room at the hotel without registering, but he did leave a valise. He had not returned.

The valise contained more clothing and another pair of shoes from Joseph Loy. Shoemaker Joseph Loy was unable to identify the suicide from the description but said he would probably recognize the man should he see the body. [73]

Sometimes, jumping off the bridge was nothing more than a spur of the moment decision fuel by alcohol. Such was the case when Patrolman Thomas Brady observed a 27-year- old printer named Patrick Sullivan hanging from a crossbeam under the promenade about two hundred feet from the New York tower. As Brady rushed toward the hanging man, Sullivan dropped down into the water, turning over several times as he fell. When he was fished out of the river Sullivan was transported to Bellevue hospital where he made a full recovery from his injuries. Sullivan said he had been drinking and that he had been suddenly seized with a desire to jump from the bridge – so he did. [74]

Sometimes it was a simple communication problem that presented the Bridge Police with problems. Officer Kane arrested a man whom he caught climbing over the promenade railing to the car tracks, believing that the man attempted to jump and commit suicide. At the police station it was found that the man was a Greek who spoke no English and had only been in America for two weeks. The man's name was Spiros Bougodes, and when an interpreter was obtained it was learned that the man was interested in the greatness of the Brooklyn Bridge and simply wished to conduct a close examination of it. He was released from custody. [75]

The Bridge police were also very familiar with jump hoaxes. It was this experience with fakers that caused Sgt. Phillips to look suspiciously at the case of Samuel Fink. The sergeant had no doubt that the 26-year-old Fink existed, and certain facts about him were clear. Fink had been employed by a marine insurance broker in New York City but had lost his position a year earlier and had been despondent since. He always dressed in the height of fashion and was addicted to gambling. Fink's health was failing as a result of his constant smoking and he was now a wreck of his former self.

One evening a conductor was standing on the platform of a bridge car when he noticed a man's coat and hat lying in the roadway near the New York tower. The conductor called to Patrolman Quilty who responded to the place indicated but found no hat or coat. It turned out that the hat and coat had been picked up by Gustave Cohen, an express driver. Cohen turned the hat and coat over to the Bridge Police, but he found a letter in the coat pocket addressed to D.J. Braun, which he did not turn over to the police. Instead, he gave the letter to a newspaper reporter. The newspaper identified D.J. Braun as Fink's brother-in- law, and the letter read as follows:

Dear Dave – When this reaches you, I will be no more. Go at once to Alice and comfort her, as she will worry when she misses me. She will find a note in the top of my trunk – With best wishes – Sam

Sergeant Phillips noted that it was an extremely peculiar letter because most bridge jumpers he had experience with didn't trouble themselves to get rid of their clothing and send best wishes to friends and family. He said that most of them were thinking only about jumping just before they take the plunge. Phillips additionally said that he was on the bridge around the time the jump supposedly occurred, and he could say confidently that it would have been impossible for any man to jump without being seen. A few days later Braun, the brother-in-law, called the Bridge Police station and told Captain Ward that Fink had been perpetrating a hoax upon him, the police, and the public.

HEROES AND VILLAINS

The history of the police in New York City is a story of heroes. Throughout this history, however, there have been numerous instances of corruption and misconduct. This rogue's gallery includes the brutality of "Clubber" Williams, Charles Becker, the only member of the department to receive the death penalty, Michael Dowd and his Long Island drug ring, and the infamous "Buddy Boys." The Bridge Police didn't have as many villains, but they did have Michael Lally.

Mike Lally was a well-known figure in New York City in the waning years of the 19th century. He was a product of the corruption of Tammany Hall and was appointed a policeman on the Brooklyn Bridge due to the influence of Alderman Patrick Divver. [76]

About eleven o'clock on a Saturday morning, a young man hobbled into the Chambers Street Hospital leaning upon the arm of a stalwart fellow who was half drunk. The young man said his name was Peter Hurley, a bartender who had accidentally shot himself in the foot. The doctors sent him to the operating room and threatened to eject his companion who wanted to stay with him. The man pulled open his coat displaying a badge and said he was a policeman. The man was finally persuaded to leave. Hurley said his friend was Michael Rorr or Michael something.

A man who identified himself as Dennis Lally, a truckman, said Hurley had accidentally shot himself with a pistol while examining the gun inside Durkin's Saloon. where he was the bartender. The man who took Hurley to the hospital, Lally said, was a Bridge Policeman named Collins who was off duty and with Hurley at the time of the accident. At the Front Street saloon, the bartender told a reporter that there was no bartender named Hurley and that no one shot themselves in the saloon, and that no one named Durkin or Lally was associated with the saloon. However, a half dozen people outside the place said that the saloon was Durkin and Lally's place.

The story going around the neighborhood was that Michael Lally was a Bridge Policeman and one of the saloon owners and also a Tammany Committeeman. Lally came into the saloon drunk on Saturday morning and ordered Hurley to dance. Hurley refused and Lally drew his revolver and again ordered Hurley to dance while pointing the gun at Hurley's feet. Hurley then refused and Lally shot him and took him to the hospital.

The infamous Michael Lally

Lally was asked about the incident while on duty at the bridge and denied everything, even though the city records listed Michael Lally as a Tammany Committee member. The saloon was listed as being owned by Dennis Lally, who Michael Lally said was no relation. [77]

Even with the publicity Lally remained on the force. Subsequently while drunk, Lally assaulted his supervisor, Roundsman Brophy. It was during the afternoon on Christmas day Roundsman Brophy noticed Lally acting boisterously at the Sands Street entrance to the bridge. He corrected Lally's behavior which prompted Lally to take off his coat and ready himself to fight Brophy, who he then kicked in the abdomen and shin. [78]

Lally also assaulted several bridge passengers, but the trustees did not remove him until he assaulted Roundsman Brophy. He even sued unsuccessfully to get his job back.

Staying true to form, Lally had an ex-assemblyman appear with him at his department trial for assaulting the roundsman, and while on suspension for this charge he was involved in another shooting.

It was on a Sunday morning at seven o'clock when a drunk Lally entered a Water Street dive called The Old Home. Lally approached the 32-year-old Italian bartender named John Delati and asked how much he owed him. Delati told Lally that he owed him nothing and to go about his business. Lally tried to hit Delati, who went to get his club kept behind the bar. Lally pulled out a revolver and shot Delati in the chest. [79]

Even though he had been dismissed from the Bridge Police force, Alderman Divver's pull saw to it that Lally did not spend any time in jail for the shooting. The newspapers picked up the case, however, and a grand jury indicted Lally, but he fled before the indictment could be served. When he returned two years later every witness could not be found or had changed their story,

The charges were dismissed when Delati suddenly changed his story. Now he said that when Lally came in and asked for a drink he told him he had nothing but soft drinks and the gave him a glass of sarsaparilla that he refused to pay for. Lally called Delati names and Delati called Lally names. Delati got his club and hit Lally. Other men came into the place and Delati was shot in the chest while Lally stood in front of him. Delati said, "If Lally had shot me

I would have known it. I have a very excitable temper and am to blame for the trouble."

The charges were dismissed even though three witnesses positively identified Lally as the shooter. The judge still dismissed the charges because the arresting officer Grogan said he could not locate the witnesses. A newspaper reporter, however, easily located the witnesses, but the witnesses also changed their stories and said other men entered the bar who may have shot Delati. The owner of The Old House at first said he would help any way he could in prosecuting Lally because he brought his already notorious establishment more notoriety. The owner then also changed his story, saying that the Italian got what he deserved and that he had no business pulling a club. [80]

Lally was also involved in numerous other assaults. On one occasion he brutally knocked down and kicked an elderly Brooklyn resident who had asked him a question. And on another occasion, he insulted and beat a young woman. Lally's political and law enforcement career was not over, however, as Divver got fellow politician John Y. McKane to employ Lally as a detective in Coney Island while Divver saw to it that Lally's name got on the city payroll as a laborer. [81]

In summing up the dismissal of charges in the Delati shooting, Lally's lawyer commented, "Lally certainly has great luck. He seems to know how to shoot with discrimination. The fatally wounded men never fail to recover and go on the stand to say that it was all their fault." [82]

Lally even held court for his well-wishers after the charges were dismissed with a newspaper article noting that the ex-bridge policeman received callers at the saloon of his father, but that these callers were not numerous seeing that Lally had three attempts of murder in four years and gone scot free

Lally was arrested for illegal electioneering but his "pull" kept handcuffs off him and got his bail lowered from $7500 to $1000. [83]

In what appeared to be ex-Patrolman Lally's last encounter with the law, hey was arrested in December 1893 pursuant to an indictment by a New York County Grand Jury for illegal electioneering in connection with actions he took at the behest of John McKane.

McKane was a powerful Brooklyn politician, especially in the Gravesend section, and along with Patrick Divver, he was one of Lally's main political benefactors. It was the election of 1893 that was McKane's undoing. The state legislature previously had passed an election reform bill that was designed to stop his practice of sitting in the Town Hall where he could eye each voter. That November he received a warning that a group of Republican reformers were planning to observe the election in Gravesend. Naturally McKane wasn't going to let it happen and instructed 150 of his henchmen armed with clubs. to make sure that no strangers approach the Town Hall. He was particularly worried because he had 6,218 voters registered when there weren't more than 1,500 legitimate voters in all six districts.

Three carriages filled with strangers approached the Town Hall at sunrise and were met by a hostile crowd of 300 men, led by fifty policemen. The reformer's leader was Colonel Alexander Bacon. When the colonel told McKane that he had an injunction for him, McKane with his hands firmly clasped behind his back, confidently proclaimed that "Injunctions don't go here." Bacon held out the paper and lunged forward to serve with it by slapping him with it on the chest and shoulders. McKane, as arrogant as ever, arrested them but not before McKane's men shoved and pushed them, knocking them down and even hitting the men with their nightsticks. They were arrested for disturbing the peace and put in a cell. McKane celebrated his latest triumph and opened the polls.

One stranger escaped and the story was carried back to the righteous editor of the Brooklyn Eagle. By noon he printed a special edition about the incident at Coney Island with the headline "Injunctions Don't Go Here!". The wire services picked up the story and by the end of the day the entire country was reading about it.

McKane was confident that the incident would blow over in a day or two. However, reformers swept into office both in the State Supreme Court, state attorney general's office and in the mayor's office of nearby Brooklyn. Worse for McKane, the reformers were howling for blood. Newly appointed assistant attorney generals summoned an extraordinary grand jury into session. [84]

When the Extraordinary Grand Jury indicted McKane they also charged many of his henchmen, including Michael Lally. This charge of illegal electioneering, added to his previous unsavory reputation made Lally's arrest more commented on than any of the 67 arrested. Even then Lally's political sway was still present, as it was suggested in the newspapers that the police were not particularly active in arresting Lally after the warrant had been issued. [85]

A final note on Michael Lally was that as a result of his indictment for illegal electioneering, he was identified by another victim. As the New York Times described, for a long time, the Reverend Mr. Kent was trying to find out who the big ruffian was who beat and bruised him severely on that morning in McKanetown. It was none other than the notorious Michael Lally now under indictment for participating in New York election frauds. Lally used to be one of McKane's special officers. [86]

Michael Lalley was in a category to himself when it came to corruption and misconduct on the Bridge Police force, but it didn't mean there weren't other isolated incidents.

In a very strange incident, the Bridge Police Station almost became the scene of a tragedy. A little after three o'clock in the afternoon Captain Ward was visited by Policeman John W. McKenna of the 1st Precinct who said he was in a search of his daughter Lillie. McKenna said he believed Bridge Police Roundsman Charles Heath had something to do with Lillie's disappearance. Heath was sent for and confronted by McKenna. He at first denied all knowledge of the girl but at Captain Ward's insisting that he tell what he knew he admitted that he had met the girl adrift in New York and had given her money to accompany him to a house of ill repute in the city where he had frequently met her. He took the matter very coolly and alluded to the girl as if he may have known where she was.

Lillie was 23-years-old and until recently lived at home. She worked on Chambers Street and walked across the bridge each day. Somehow, she became acquainted with Heath. Six weeks earlier Lillie told her father she had gotten a job as a companion and dressmaker and that she would be living with her patron at an address on Lexington Avenue. Mckenna saw nothing strange but six weeks later he was on vacation in New York and ran into a friend who said he saw Lillie enter an evil place in the Bowery in the company of a stranger. The address on Lexington Avenue didn't exist and his investigation revealed the man to be Heath.

Heath admitted being intimate with the young woman, but he claimed that she was of loose character and denied having induced her to leave her home. [87]

Mckenna became very excited and in a sudden burst of fury he whipped a revolver from his pocket and pointed it at the roundsman. Captain Ward sprang between them and wrenched the weapon from McKenna's hand and succeeded in getting him into the station where he soon became calmer and departed. Superintendent Martin was informed of the case, and he promptly dismissed Heath from the force.

Heath was 55 years old and had been on the bridge force since it opened. He had formerly been with the New York Police and was widower without children.

Mckenna, who was over 50 years of age had been with the Brooklyn Police for twelve years. He said he would have shot Heath if not for Captain Ward.

Heath came one last time to the bridge station with his head hanging low. The other policemen avoided him and he did not seem happy. He delivered his uniform and shield and received $40 dollars due him. [88]

Then there was the case of Bridge Patrolman Joseph Smith who was charged with murder in 1891. Newspaper articles reported that Smith's sister, Ms. Wells ran a boarding house in Paterson, New Jersey. Smith and his family were staying at the house while he was on vacation from the bridge force. Smith returned to the house after an evening of drinking and engaged in a verbal argument with his sister regarding his excessive drinking. At some point, Smith struck his sister.

Minutes later, another resident of the house, John McElbery, while passing Smith on the basement stairs, made a remark to Smith which caused Smith to hit McElbery in the jaw with a blackjack. The force broke McElbery's jaw, rendered him unconscious and he fell down the stairs fracturing his skull at the top of his spine causing his death.

In an attempt to cover-up the crime, McElbery's body was removed from the house and left in the street where a passerby noticed it and notified a police officer. The police quickly determined the truth and sought Smith who had "hastily gathered his family and baggage together and made a hurried departure." No further information was disclosed.

Just like police today, sometimes bridge officers were falsely accused of misconduct. As illustrated in this story, it didn't appear too difficult in the late 19th century to provide a false name to the police. A man arraigned in the

Tombs Police Court said his name was John Burns, a Bridge Police Officer. He was charged with disorderly conduct towards a young woman, Lizzie McGreevy. Burns was drunk on a ferry boat and made insulting remarks to the girl. The girl called a policeman when the boat docked, and Burns was arrested. The problem was that Burns said he was never on the ferry. He never met McGreevy and lived in Brooklyn, not at the Manhattan address given by the arrested man. He also said he had not been in Manhattan in months, and no one named John Burns lived at the address given [89].

Though not usually involving murder and shootings, news articles reported that complaints of misconduct against Bridge Policemen were such frequent occurrences as to warrant the belief that not all of them were unfounded.

The most frequent offenses were rudeness and brutality on the platforms where the cars start. One article pointed out that the Bridge Police seemed to have a code of thou shalt and thou shalt not known to the uniformed ruffians but not known to the thousands they abuse. Any of these infractions of the hidden laws the police consider a fair excuse for the exercise of their power, and they are not gentle about it. They seem to go by the principle that the people are generally disorderly, law defying, and to be restrained only by the heavy hand of the law – hence, the hurrying businessman who puts a foot on a car platform at the time the signal sounds for starting, must be knocked around the station and abused.

The article cited the example of a 56-year-old woman who died after passing out when the police were roughing up her husband who still had his foot on the platform when the gong sounded. The brutal policemen who do not seem to know how to deport themselves should be disciplined and displaced. [90]

Another odd complaint was the shock expressed by citizens at the open-necked costume of sailors who crossed the bridge with their girl companions, and how the Bridge Police were allowing this condition to exist because they were frequently off post. [91]

As Bridge Policeman John H. Bishop found out, it was important to know who you were dealing with while on patrol. Bishop had been with the force for nine years with only one previous offense on his record for having his shoes shined while on post for which he was fined $5. In this case Bishop was charged with conduct unbecoming an officer to bridge Vice President Skinner.

There had been a crowd of noisy bootblacks and newsboys assembled at the Sands Street entrance impeding pedestrians. Skinner ordered Bishop to disperse the boys and was met with a point-blank refusal and an "intolerant stare."

Skinner stated that he was the vice president of the bridge and was ordering Bishop to chase these boys away. Bishop realized his mistake and immediately apologized and complied with the order. Later Bishop said he had been ordered to protect the telephone box in the station and to watch for accidents on the stairs and he didn't want to leave his post at the direction of member of the public. Captain Ward said bishop was one of his best officers. [92]

Even though Captain Ward stood behind Patrolman Bishop, the same couldn't be said for four other bridge policemen who the captain said committed one of the most "serious" violations of bridge rules ever.

Patrolmen Christopher Ferris, Adam Klein, William McEntee, and Thomas Rice were charged with congregating in the bridge tower hut at 2:30 am.

Ferris had one prior disciplinary action when he was fined 5-days' pay for being off post. He pled guilty to the current charge with no excuse.

Klein, who had a good record, said he went into the hut because he had a sick shoulder.

Rice arrived for the trial 40-minutes late stating that he was detained at the room of his tonsorial artist. I had to look that term up and found out he had been at the barber shop, Rice, who had received charges several times before, said he went into the hut to get warm.

McEntee arrived 30 minutes late for the trial. He said he went into the hut to eat a sandwich.

I could not find the disposition of these charges but if sitting inside the hut on the bridge was the most serious violation of bridge rules ever, I am glad I was not a Bridge Policeman. [93]

Even Captain Ward was not immune from allegations of misconduct. The captain was accused by Trustee C.A. Henriques of violating one of the regulations governing the force which prohibited the raising of a fund for political or any other purpose. Neither Captain Ward or the other members of the bridge force denied that a sum of money was raised by the police, but they said it was for the purpose of paying counsel, and that when the matter was brought to Captain Ward's attention, the money was returned to the donors at his direction. Captain Ward commented that if Mr. Henriques had not been so hasty and had investigated before acting, he would have seen that he had no hand in raising the money. Captain Ward went on to say that he believed the men had just as much right to look out for their own interests as the trustees When the trustees' interests were threatened, they had the bridge's counsel to represent them, yet they questioned the right of the police to pay their own money for the same kind of protection. [94]

At Captain Ward's trial, Mr. Henriques summoned five members of the Bridge Police force as witnesses but was unsuccessful in obtaining any testimony to support his charges. All the witnesses testified they had contributed $1.10 for their own legal defense fund, but that Captain Ward had nothing to do with the collection of the funds and that it was the captain who directed the monies to be returned to the contributors. With that failed testimony Mr. Henriques tried to get the witnesses to acknowledge they had contributed $1.75 towards buying a diamond ring as a gift for Captain Ward. Mr. Henriques received no admissions for this line of questioning and Captain Ward was eventually exonerated of the charges. [95]

So far, all the stories regarding Bridge Policemen have been negative. Frankly, the negative stories were primarily all I could find in my research. I am sure there were many heroic acts performed by Bridge Policemen, but I could not find any documented. I also could not find any information regarding any Bridge Policemen killed in the line of duty, although I did find one officer who came very close.

Between seven and eight o'clock one evening Bridge Officer Meredith was patrolling near the Brooklyn tower when he passed a woman dressed in black and heavily veiled. She was walking very slowly and there was something in her appearance which led the officer to turn around. As he did so he saw the barrel of a pistol glistening in the electric light and pointed directly at his head. The woman uttered a cry of disappointed rage and advancing on the officer tried in vain to disentangle the hammer of the weapon, which had become caught in her veil. She was disarmed and taken into custody. She said her name was Annie Garvey and that she had gone on the bridge for the purpose of shooting Meredith, who she said had ruined her. She was loud in her regrets and cursed the luck that had made the hammer of her pistol catch in her veil just as she had pulled the trigger.

Garvey said that several months earlier she had met Meredith on the bridge and became acquainted with him. She was a single, 26-year-old dressmaker and Meredith had represented himself as a widower with one child. He asked her to live with him and under the promise that he would marry her, she consented. They took a room, but he deserted her in a week. When she went to see him on the bridge, he abused her and arrested her. When she promised the captain she would not bother Meredith, she was released.

Meredith admitted living with her but denied agreeing to marry her. He was not living with his wife when he first met Garvey. Meredith said Garvey had continually harassed him and went to the office of the bridge police a week earlier and threatened to make trouble. Garvey said that she purchased the pistol – a small five-chambered revolver-loaded it herself and fired one shot out her back window before proceeding to the bridge in order to ensure the weapon worked. Meredith referred to her as a woman of loose character. [96]

This next case involved no heroics, but it was a Bridge Policeman being injured in the line of duty. Officer Patrick Mulligan, of the Brooklyn Bridge Police was seriously hurt one afternoon in stepping off a train that was leaving the New York side. Trains were hauled by locomotives during a part of the afternoon because of the temporary stopping of the cable for repairs to machinery. Great crowds of people collected in consequence and extraordinary vigilance was necessary on the part of the officers to maintain order and prevent accidents. Officer Mulligan boarded the front car of the 2:20 train to prevent the impatient people from overcrowding the platform, and in doing so, struck against a wooden horse and some other scaffolding that happened to be there. The momentum which he had acquired from the train was so great that he carried the horse with him off the platform to the roadway below. His head struck against the horse and his right foot fell under the wheels of the train and three toes were crushed. He was not noticed for the moment, and it was not until the train had passed out of the station that two other officers saw him lying unconscious. They immediately picked him up and carried him to the engine house. An ambulance was called and physicians dressed the wounds. Officer Mulligan was 38-years old and married and had been on the force for three years. [97]

The tragedy of suicide is an unfortunate reality in the police profession, and the Bridge Police were not immune. Frederick Richards, a member of the Brooklyn Bridge police force committed suicide in his home on the third floor of 102 Ludlow Street. Richards was once discharged from the bridge force for intoxication and had to use extraordinary influence to get reinstated. The lesson did not serve him for he got drunk while attending the funeral of a brother officer who died of pneumonia. He was unfit for duty on two days and was suspended. He feared dismissal and his young wife urged him keep sober, but he continued to drink, and at 5 o'clock in the afternoon he went into his bedroom. He had just been told by his wife that if he did not do better, she would leave him, and after going into the kitchen he said, "you will have no more trouble with me." A few minutes later he began to groan, and it was found it he had taken oxalic acid kept to clean his uniform buttons. Physicians were summoned but they could do nothing for him, and he died. He was once a member of the New York Police and was dismissed for intoxication. His wife said that he often threatened to commit suicide because he was tired of life, threatening to either jump off the bridge or blow his brains out. [98]

I wish I could have found a story of a Bridge Policeman cited for valor in the line of duty, but the closest I could find was Edward Wiggins whose heroics occurred years before he was with the bridge force.

As a young man Wiggins enlisted in the Navy and during the Civil War and was coxswain on the Union ship Iroquois. He served under Admiral Farragaut during the invasion of New Orleans, and when the fleet landed Wiggins led the charge on the city and planted the first American Flag on Canal Street.

In 1894 Congressman John Michael Clancy submitted Wiggins, then a 55-year-old roundsman with the Bridge Police, for the Medal of Honor for his actions during the Civil War. Wiggins never received the award, but it is an honor to just be considered for the medal. [99]

EDWARD WIGGINS.

THE END

New Year's Day 1898, the weather predicted light snow in the morning, a normal condition for New York City in the winter. Something very unusual, however, had occurred at the stroke of midnight. When the new year rolled in, Manhattan, Brooklyn, Queens, and Staten Island, officially consolidated to become the Greater City of New York.

This same January 1st saw the birth of the New York City Police Department as eighteen separate police departments in the area merged into a single police force of 6,396 members. Although the bulk of the new NYPD's members came from the New York Police, some of the other jurisdictions were the Brooklyn Police Department, Long Island City Police Department, Park Police, Telegraph Bureau, Richmond Police Department, as well as several departments from sections of Brooklyn and Queens. Also merged into the NYPD was the Brooklyn Bridge Police Department.

In the weeks preceding the new year, the smaller departments added members to their compliment and promoted others in an effort to increase their ranks and standing in the merged force.

The members of the Bridge Police force waited with considerable anxiety for the outcome of a December 26th Board of Trustees meeting. This would be the last meeting of the trustees before the bridge force was merged into the new NYPD and the question as to whether six members of the bridge force would be promoted was still not settled. Several weeks earlier the trustees had promoted Roundsman Brophy to Sergeant and Patrolman Brady to Roundsman. Since that time, however, nothing had been done regarding the other promotions, even though Captain Ward was pushing for the promotions. He argued that the promotions would be a simple act of justice as these men were due promotions years earlier. He further stated that if the promotions were not made before the merger, these men would have to wait years for the possibility of being promoted. Captain Ward continued that the promotions made sense operationally in the newly organized department. He said that the bridge force currently consisted of 98-men, one of who was a captain, with three sergeants and three roundsmen. He continued that the force was divided into three platoons with a sergeant and roundsman assigned to each platoon, so to bring the bridge force up to the proper staffing levels of the new NYPD three sergeants and three roundsmen should be added to the bridge force. [100] Although the argument made perfect sense, for an unstated reason, C.A. Henriques, Vice President of the Board, would not agree to the promotions. [101

In the end it didn't matter because it was later discovered that the actual number of police officers in the new NYPD exceeded the number allotted by the Charter resulting in the termination of these extra men. To manage the new NYPD a bi-partisan Police Board consisting of four commissioners was appointed. [102]

After a brief fifteen-year existence the Brooklyn Bridge Police Department was swept away into the sands of history. The bridge police, however, did not just disappear with a snap of the fingers on January 1, 1898. It seemed to be a similar situation to what I experienced when the Transit Police Department ceased to exist on April 2, 1995. On April 1st I was assigned to District 20 in the Transit Police Department. The next day nothing really changed. I was still working in District 20, only now District 20 was part of the new NYPD Transit Bureau. People still referred to the cops in the subway as transit cops and still do today as a matter of fact.

In 1898 the Brooklyn Bridge Police still patrolled the bridge as part of the NYPD. Captain Ward still managed the bridge force until he retired during September of the same year. At that time Captain John Eason of the Vernon Avenue station was picked to succeed Ward, with the bridge command becoming part of the First Inspection District of Manhattan. [103]

After the Transit Police merged into the NYPD in 1995 there was a public concern that the manpower policing the subways would gradually be shifted to conditions on the street. The same thing happened with the Brooklyn Bridge. Five years after the bridge force was consolidated into the new NYPD the police commissioner divorced the police department wholly from bridge management. By consolidating the Bridge Police with the City Hall, Manhattan Precinct, wiping out for all intents and purposes the Fourth Precinct which had sole charge of policing the bridge. [104]

The idea for the move was because it was believed that the traffic on the bridge would be under better control if the man in charge of the City Hall station had something to do with it. The cops of the City Hall Precinct had been drilled in the management of street traffic on Park Row and thoroughfares near the bridge. [105]

Some changes took much longer. Finally, in 1918 the Bridge Police Squad moved from the cellar of 179 Washington Street to one floor up. They had been in the cellar since the bridge opened in 1883. The commanding officer Edward Toole now had his own room in the sunlight. This was the first ttime the operation was above ground since its foundation under Captain James Ward. [106]

The Brooklyn Bridge Police existed from May 1883 to midnight on December 31, 1897. While the history of the force was not stellar, extraordinary, or lengthy, it nonetheless is part of the history of New York City policing.

Bibliography

1. Joseph A. Williams, The Police riot of 1857, The History Channel, https://www.history.com/news/police-riot-1857-mayor-corruption, retrieved 4/1/22.

2. Kevin Walsh, Street Easy Reads, 11/27/18, https://streeteasy.com/blog/brooklyn-bridge/, retrieved 4/1/22

3. People ex rel. Rae v. York, 1898, Casetext, https://casetext.com/case/people-ex-rel-rae-v-york, retrieved 3/28/22.

4. Untitled, New York Times, 6/16/1889, https://timesmachine.nytimes.com/timesmachine/1895/06/16/102462269.pdf?pdf_redirect=true&ip=0, retrieved 3/14/22

5. Nichols, Mark, Daily Writing Tips, 20 Slang Terms for Law Enforcement Personnel

6. The William Steinway Diary, Smithstonian Institute Libraries, https://americanhistory.si.edu/steinwaydiary/annotations/?id=1996, retrieved 3/2/22

7. Untitled, The Brooklyn Daily Eagle, 5/29/1883, p3, https://bklyn.newspapers.com/image/50431577/?terms=%22bridge%20police%22&match=1, retrieved 5/2/22

8. Untitled, New York Times, 5/24/1883, https://timesmachine.nytimes.com/timesmachine/1883/05/24/102823242.html?pageNumber=1 retrieved 5/8/22.

9. McNamara, Robert. "Brooklyn Bridge Disaster." ThoughtCo, Aug. 28, 2020, thoughtco.com/brooklyn-bridge-disaster-1773696.

10. Untitled, The Brooklyn Daily Eagle, 6/6/1883, p2

11. Untitled, The Brooklyn Daily Eagle, 6/5/1883, p3

12. Untitled, The Brooklyn Daily Eagle, 7/14/1883, p4

13. Untitled, New York Times, 6/2/1883, https://timesmachine.nytimes.com/timesmachine/1883/06/02/102826486.pdf?pdf_redirect=true&ip=0, retrieved 5/4/22

14. 130 years Ago, Elephants Solved Panic on the Brooklyn Bridge, New York Historical Society Museum and Library, May 29, 2014.

15. Untitled, The Brooklyn Daily Eagle, 6/12/1894, p6

16. Lardner and Repetto, NYPD: A City and its Police, Owl Books, New York, p62.

17. Untitled, The Brooklyn Daily Eagle, 5/3/1896, p4

18. Untitled, The Brooklyn Daily Eagle, 5/3/1896,p4

19. Untitled, The Brooklyn Union, 9/23/1884, p8

20. Untitled, The Brooklyn Daily Eagle, 12/1/1886, https://bklyn.newspapers.com/image/50333951/?terms=%22bridge%20police%22&match=1 retrieved 5/3/22

21. Untitled, The Standard Union, 12/9/1889, p1

22. Untitled, The Brooklyn Daily Eagle, 5/3/1896, p5

23. Untitled, The New York Times, 6/16/1895, https://timesmachine.nytimes.com/timesmachine/1895/06/16/102462269.pdf?pdf_redirect=true&ip=0, retrieved 4/21/22

24. Untitled, The New York Times, 5/22/1883, 102822662.pdf (nytimes.com)[3],retrieved 4/28/22

25. Untitled, The Brooklyn Daily Eagle, 4/19/1889, p4

26. Mount Vernon Organization,https://www.mountvernon.org/george-washington/the-first-president/centennial-celebration/ retrieved 3/31/22

27. Untitled, The New York Times, 4/9/1889, TimesMachine: April 9, 1889 - NYTimes.com[4], retrieved 3/30/22

28. Untitled, The New York Times, 4/16/1889, 106345726.pdf (nytimes.com)[5], retrieved 3/3/22

29. Untitled, The Brooklyn Daily Eagle, 6/15/1894, p1

30. Untitled, The Brooklyn Daily Eagle, 10/15/1885, https://bklyn.newspapers.com/image/50406582/?terms=%22bridge%20police%22&match=1, retrieved 4/10/22

31. Untitled, The New York Times, 6/12/1894, https://timesmachine.nytimes.com/timesmachine/1894/06/12/106099549.pdf?pdf_redirect=true&ip=0, retrieved 5/5/22

32. Untitled, The Brooklyn Daily Eagle, 5/3/1896, p1

33. Untitled, The Brooklyn Daily Eagle, 6/12/1894, p1.

34. Untitled, The Brooklyn Daily Eagle, 6/12/1894, p1.

---

3. https://timesmachine.nytimes.com/timesmachine/1883/05/22/102822662.pdf?pdf_redirect=true&ip=0

4. https://timesmachine.nytimes.com/timesmachine/1889/04/09/issue.html

5. https://timesmachine.nytimes.com/timesmachine/1889/04/16/106345726.pdf?pdf_redirect=true&ip=0

35. Work of the Bridge Police, The Brooklyn Daily Eagle, 12/1/1886, p2.

36. Untitled, Standard Union, 12/9/1889, p1

37. Untitled, The New York Times, 6/27/1883, https://timesmachine.nytimes.com/timesmachine/1883/06/27/103437511.pdf?pdf_redirect=true&ip=0, retrieved 5/15/22

38. Untitled, The Brooklyn Daily Eagle, 3/6/1890, https://bklyn.newspapers.com/image/60731221/?terms=%22bridge%20police%22&match=1, retrieved 5/1/22

39. Untitled, The New York Times, 2/5/1886, 106181318.pdf (nytimes.com)[6], retrieved 5/1/22.

40. Untitled, The Brooklyn Daily Eagle, 10/7/1884, https://bklyn.newspapers.com/image/60776276/?terms=%22bridge%20police%22&match=1, retrieved 5/10/22

41. Untitled, The New York Times, 12/6/1883, https://timesmachine.nytimes.com/timesmachine/1883/12/06/issue.html?auth=login-email, retrieved 4/27/22

42. Untitled, The New York Times, 1/5/1884, https://timesmachine.nytimes.com/timesmachine/1884/01/05/issue.html, retrieved 4/5/22

43. Schoenberg, Phillip, If you Believe that, I have a bridge to Sell you, NYC Walks Blog 35, The Brooklyn Bridge, 2018

44. Untitled, The New York Times, 4/3/1885, https://timesmachine.nytimes.com/timesmachine/1885/04/21/102971967.html?pageNumber=5, retrieved 5/11/22

45. Untitled, The Brooklyn Daily Eagle, 7/17/1897, https://bklyn.newspapers.com/image/50369984/?terms=%22bridge%20police%22&match=1, retrieved 5/12/22

46. Untitled, The New York Times, 12/18/1883, https://timesmachine.nytimes.com/timesmachine/1883/12/18/106267890.pdf?pdf_redirect=true&ip=0, retrieved 3/26/22

47. Untitled, The Brooklyn Daily Eagle, 2/11/1902,

---

6. https://timesmachine.nytimes.com/timesmachine/1886/02/05/106181318.pdf?pdf_redirect=true&ip=0

https://bklyn.newspapers.com/image/
50415737/?terms=%22bridge%20police%22&match=1, retrieved 3/
15/22

48. Untitled, The Brooklyn Daily eagle, 6/13/1904,
    https://bklyn.newspapers.com/image/
    53111880/?terms=%22bridge%20police%22&match=1, retrieved 3/
    16/22

49. Untitled, The Brooklyn Daily Eagle, 1/29/1885,
    https://bklyn.newspapers.com/image/
    50425753/?terms=%22bridge%20police%22&match=1, retrieved
    3/17/22

50. Untitled, The New York Times, 2/12/1885,
    https://timesmachine.nytimes.com/timesmachine/1885/02/12/
    106298591.pdf?pdf_redirect=true&ip=0, retrieved 3/17/22

51. Untitled, The Brooklyn Daily Eagle, 1/12/1897,
    https://bklyn.newspapers.com/image/
    50474813/?terms=%22bridge%20police%22&match=1, retrieved 4/
    10/22

52. Untitled, The Brooklyn Daily Eagle, 10/23/1886, p6.

53. Untitled, The Brooklyn Daily Eagle, 1/30/1884,
    https://bklyn.newspapers.com/image/
    50342463/?terms=%22bridge%20police%22&match=1, retrieved
    4/20/22

54. DeLong, George W, Naval History and Heritage Command.

55. Untitled, The Brooklyn Daily Eagle, 2/28/1884,
    https://bklyn.newspapers.com/image/
    50342920/?terms=%22bridge%20police%22&match=1, retrieved
    5/5/22

56. Untitled, The Brooklyn Daily eagle, 11/24/1884,
    https://bklyn.newspapers.com/image/
    60780704/?terms=%22bridge%20police%22&match=1, retrieved
    3/1/22

57. Untitled, The Brooklyn Daily Eagle, 3/25/1885, p5.

58. Misrahi's Lost Diamonds, The Brooklyn Daily Eagle, 8/3/1897, p12.

59. Untitled, The Standard Union, 8/9/1900, p12.

60. Gormley, Larry, Because it's There, Ohio State University, Department of History.

61. Simonovski, Nikola, Robert Odlum, The First Man to Jump off the Brooklyn Bridge to prove people did not die simply from falling through the air, 4/4/18

62. Steve Brodie Took a Chance and Made a Jump, The Brooklyn Daily Eagle, 5/24/1933, p32

63. Untitled, The Brooklyn Public Library, 6/19/21, https://www.bklynlibrary.org/blog/2021/07/19/steve-brodie-jumped, retrieved 5/15/22.

64. An Unsolved Riddle, Did Brodie Jump?, The Brooklyn Daily Eagle, 4/4/1930, p21.

65. Old Bridge Cop Upholds Muldoon In Brodie Case, The Brooklyn Daily Eagle, 4/8/1930, p1, https://bklyn.newspapers.com/image/59843401/?terms=%22Bridge%20police%22&match=1, retrieved 5/1/22

66. Says Brodie Told him he never Jumped Bridge, Brooklyn Daily Eagle, 4/7/1930, p17

67. Untitled, The Brooklyn Daily Eagle, 8/30/1895, p1.

68. Untitled, The New York Times, 8/31/1895, p9

69. Untitled, The New York Times, 5/29/1885, https://timesmachine.nytimes.com/timesmachine/1885/05/29/103020733.pdf?pdf_redirect=true&ip=0, retrieved 5/2/22

70. Untitled, The New York Times, 4/4/1893, https://timesmachine.nytimes.com/timesmachine/1893/04/04/106818483.pdf?pdf_redirect=true&ip=0, retrieved 5/6/22

71. Untitled, The New York Times, 11/28/1894, https://timesmachine.nytimes.com/timesmachine/1894/11/28/106882435.pdf?pdf_redirect=true&ip=0, retrieved 4/11/22

72. Untitled, The New York Times, 6/16/1885, 109781854.pdf (nytimes.com)[7], retrieved 5/13/22

73. Untitled, The New York Times, 6/18/1900,

---

7. https://timesmachine.nytimes.com/timesmachine/1885/06/16/109781854.pdf?pdf_redirect=true&ip=0

https://timesmachine.nytimes.com/timesmachine/1900/06/18/ 102435539.pdf?pdf_redirect=true&ip=0, retrieved 4/19/22

74. Untitled, The Standard Union, 6/15/1896, p5.

75. He was not a Bridge Jumper, The Standard Union, 8/3/1896, p4.

76. The Civil Service Chronicle, Volume 1 and 2, https://books.google.com/ books?id=QCg5AQAAMAAJ&pg=RA1-PA123&lpg=RA1-PA123&dq=p [8], retrieved 5/1/22

77. Untitled, The Sun, 11/19/1889, 19 Nov 1889, Page 5 - The Sun at Newspapers.com[9], retrieved 5/6/22

78. Untitled, The Brooklyn Daily Eagle, 1/5/1891, 05 Jan 1891, Page 6 - The Brooklyn Daily Eagle at Newspapers.com[10], retrieved 4/23/22

79. Untitled, The Evening World, 2/16/1881, p1,

80. Untitled, The Evening World, 2/16/1881, p1

81. The Civil Service Chronicle, Volume 1 and 2, https://books.google.com/ books?id=QCg5AQAAMAAJ&pg=RA1-PA123&lpg=RA1-PA123&dq=p

---

8. https://books.google.com/ books?id=QCg5AQAAMAAJ&pg=RA1-PA123&lpg=RA1-PA123&dq=patrick+divver+michael+lally &source=bl&ots=cQXHWEcdvq&sig=ACfU3U1ikPSfcej3IUAQaXU5Gohn6QjDbg&hl=en&sa=X& ved=2ahUKEwjU29DYiK73AhUIgXIEHTYiBGQQ6AF6BAgCEAM#v_43ec3e5dee6e706af7766fffea5 12721_onepage_6cff047854f19ac2aa52aac51bf3af4a_q_43ec3e5dee6e706af7766fffea512721_patrick_0b cef9c45bd8a48eda1b26eb0c61c869_20divver_0bcef9c45bd8a48eda1b26eb0c61c869_20michael_0bcef9c 45bd8a48eda1b26eb0c61c869_20lally_6cff047854f19ac2aa52aac51bf3af4a_f_43ec3e5dee6e706af7766fff ea512721_false

9. https://www.newspapers.com/image/186251436/?terms=michael%20lally&match=1

10. https://www.newspapers.com/image/50470365/?terms=michael%20lally&match=1

11. https://books.google.com/ books?id=QCg5AQAAMAAJ&pg=RA1-PA123&lpg=RA1-PA123&dq=patrick+divver+michael+lally &source=bl&ots=cQXHWEcdvq&sig=ACfU3U1ikPSfcej3IUAQaXU5Gohn6QjDbg&hl=en&sa=X& ved=2ahUKEwjU29DYiK73AhUIgXIEHTYiBGQQ6AF6BAgCEAM#v_43ec3e5dee6e706af7766fffea5 12721_onepage_6cff047854f19ac2aa52aac51bf3af4a_q_43ec3e5dee6e706af7766fffea512721_patrick_0b cef9c45bd8a48eda1b26eb0c61c869_20divver_0bcef9c45bd8a48eda1b26eb0c61c869_20michael_0bcef9c 45bd8a48eda1b26eb0c61c869_20lally_6cff047854f19ac2aa52aac51bf3af4a_f_43ec3e5dee6e706af7766fff

[11] retrieved 5/1/22

82. Untitled, New York Herald, 2/17/1891, p8

83. Untitled, New York Daily Tribune, 12/29/1893, p4. 29 Dec 1893, Page 4 - New-York Tribune at Newspapers.com[12] retrieved 4/4/22

84. Stanton, Jeffrey, Coney Island – John McKane, 1997

85. Untitled, The New York Times, 12/28/1893, 109717001.pdf (nytimes.com)[13] retrieved 3/30/22

86. Untitled, The New York Times, 1/2/1894, TimesMachine: January 2, 1894 - NYTimes.com[14] retrieved 4/1/22

87. Untitled, The New York Times, 7/18/1884, 106281363.pdf (nytimes.com)[15] retrieved 4/16/22

88. Untitled, The Daily Brooklyn Eagle, 7/17/1884, p4.

89. Untitled, The New York Times, 1/24/1893, 106860957.pdf (nytimes.com)[16] retrieved 5/5/22

90. Untitled, The Standard Union, 9/17/1891, p2.

91. Untitled, The Daily Brooklyn Eagle, 8/17/1905, p5.

92. Untitled, The Standard Union, 8/20/1894, p1.

93. Untitled, The Standard Union, 11/21/1890, p1.

94. Untitled, The Daily Brooklyn Eagle, 5/8/1896, p16

95. Henriques Charges Against Ward Fell Through, The Standard Union, 5/11/1896, p1.

96. Untitled, The New York Times, 12/9/ 1883,https://timesmachine.nytimes.com/timesmachine/1883/12/ 09/106265900.pdf?pdf_redirect=true&ip=0 retrieved 4/14/22

97. Untitled, The New York Times, 7/21/1886, https://timesmachine.nytimes.com/timesmachine/1886/07/21/ 109786789.pdf?pdf_redirect=true&ip=0 retrieved 5/10/22

98. Untitled, The New York Times, 1/14/1887, TimesMachine: January 14, 1887 - NYTimes.com[17] retrieved 4/20/22

---

ea512721_false

12. https://www.newspapers.com/image/85529733/?terms=michael%20lally&match=1

13. https://timesmachine.nytimes.com/timesmachine/1893/12/28/109717001.pdf?pdf_redirect=true&ip=0

14. https://timesmachine.nytimes.com/timesmachine/1894/01/02/106091896.html?pageNumber=9

15. https://timesmachine.nytimes.com/timesmachine/1884/07/18/106281363.pdf?pdf_redirect=true&ip=0

16. https://timesmachine.nytimes.com/timesmachine/1893/01/24/106860957.pdf?pdf_redirect=true&ip=0

99.   Untitled, The Brooklyn Daily Eagle, 4/15/1894,
      https://bklyn.newspapers.com/image/
      50352071/?terms=%22bridge%20police%22&match=1, retrieved
      5/1/22

100. Untitled, The Brooklyn Daily Eagle, 12/26/1897,p28

101. Henriques Tries to Holp up Promotions, The Brooklyn Daily eagle,
      12/26/1897, p28

102. Whalen and Doorey, NYCOP.com, 2000, http://www.nycop.com/
      Stories/Aug_00/The_Birth_of_the_NYPD/
      body_the_birth_of_the_nypd.html, retrieved 5/1/22

103. Untitled, The Brooklyn Daily Eagle, 9/23/1898,
      https://bklyn.newspapers.com/image/
      50339330/?terms=%22bridge%20police%22&match=1, retrieved
      4/18/22

104. Untitled, The Brooklyn Daily Eagle, 4/25/1903, p22.

105. Untitled, The Brooklyn Daily Eagle, 4/26/1903, p3.

106. Untitled, The Brooklyn Daily Eagle, 7/21/1918,
      https://bklyn.newspapers.com/image/
      54538416/?terms=%22bridge%20police%22&match=1, retrieved 4/
      1/22

---

17. https://timesmachine.nytimes.com/timesmachine/1887/01/14/104003993.html?pageNumber=2